CB126760

Jack C. Richards & Chuck Sandy

Passages

Third Edition

1A

Student's Book with eBook

CAMBRIDGE UNIVERSITY PRESS

CAMBRIDGE
UNIVERSITY PRESS

University Printing House, Cambridge CB2 8BS, United Kingdom

One Liberty Plaza, 20th Floor, New York, NY 10006, USA

477 Williamstown Road, Port Melbourne, VIC 3207, Australia

314–321, 3rd Floor, Plot 3, Splendor Forum, Jasola District Centre, New Delhi – 110025, India

103 Penang Road, #05-06/07, Visioncrest Commercial, Singapore 238467

Cambridge University Press is part of the University of Cambridge.

It furthers the University's mission by disseminating knowledge in the pursuit of education, learning and research at the highest international levels of excellence.

www.cambridge.org
Information on this title: www.cambridge.org/9781009040761

First published 1998
Second edition 2008
Third edition 2015
Update to Third edition published 2021

20 19 18 17 16 15 14 13 12 11 10 9 8 7 6 5 4 3 2 1

Printed in Poland by Opolgraf

A catalogue record for this publication is available from the British Library

ISBN 978-1-009-04061-7 Student's Book 1 with eBook
ISBN 978-1-009-04076-1 Student's Book 1A with eBook
ISBN 978-1-009-04082-2 Student's Book 1B with eBook
ISBN 978-1-009-04086-0 Student's Book 1 with Digital Pack
ISBN 978-1-009-04087-7 Student's Book 1A with Digital Pack
ISBN 978-1-009-04088-4 Student's Book 1B with Digital Pack
ISBN 978-1-107-62725-3 Workbook 1
ISBN 978-1-107-62718-5 Workbook 1A
ISBN 978-1-107-62720-8 Workbook 1B
ISBN 978-1-107-62768-0 Teacher's Edition 1 with Assessment Audio
ISBN 978-1-107-62754-3 Class Audio 1
ISBN 978-1-009-04089-1 Full Contact 1 with Digital Pack
ISBN 978-1-009-04090-7 Full Contact 1A with Digital Pack
ISBN 978-1-009-04091-4 Full Contact 1B with Digital Pack
ISBN 978-1-107-62762-8 DVD 1
ISBN 978-1-107-66626-9 Presentation Plus 1

Additional resources for this publication at cambridgeone.org

Art direction, book design, layout services, and photo research: Q2A / Bill Smith
Audio production: John Marshall Media
Video production: Steadman Productions

Authors' Acknowledgments

A great number of people contributed to the development of *Passages Third Edition*. Particular thanks are owed to the following reviewers and institutions, as their insights and suggestions have helped define the content and format of the third edition:

Paulo A. Machado, Rio de Janeiro, Brazil; Simone C. Wanguestel, Niterói, Brazil; Athiná Arcadinos Leite, **ACBEU**, Salvador, Brazil; Lauren Osowski, **Adult Learning Center**, Nashua, NH, USA; Brenda Victoria, **AIF System**, Santiago, Dominican Republic; Alicia Mitchell-Boncquet, **ALPS Language School**, Seattle, WA, USA; Scott C. Welsh, **Arizona State University**, Tempe, AZ, USA; Silvia Corrêa, **Associação Alumni**, São Paulo, Brazil; Henrick Oprea, **Atlantic Idiomas**, Brasília, Brazil; Márcia Lima, **B.A. English School**, Goiânia, Brazil; Carlos Andrés Mejía Gómez, **BNC Centro Colombo Americano Pereira**, Pereira, Colombia; Tanja Jakimoska, **Brava Training**, Rio de Janeiro, Brazil; Paulo Henrique Gomes de Abreu, **Britannia International English**, Rio de Janeiro, Brazil; Gema Kuri Rodríguez, **Business & English**, Puebla, Mexico; Isabela Villas Boas, **Casa Thomas Jefferson**, Brasília, Brazil; Inara Lúcia Castillo Couto, **CEL-LEP**, São Paulo, Brazil; Ana Cristina Hebling Meira, **Centro Cultural Brasil-Estados Unidos**, Campinas, Brazil; Juliana Costa da Silva, **Centro de Cultura Anglo Americana**, Rio de Janeiro, Brazil; Heriberto Díaz Vázquez, **Centro de Investigación y Docencia Económicas**, Mexico City, Mexico; D. L. Dorantes-Salas, **Centro de Investigaciones Biológicas del Noroeste**, La Paz, Mexico; Elizabeth Carolina Llatas Castillo, **Centro Peruano Americano El Cultural**, Trujillo-La Libertad, Peru; Márcia M. A. de Brito, **Chance Language Center**, Rio de Janeiro, Brazil; Rosalinda Heredia, **Colegio Motolinia**, San Juan del Río, Mexico; Maria Regina Pereira Filgueiras, **College Language Center**, Londrina, Brazil; Lino Mendoza Rodriguez, **Compummunicate**, Izúcar de Matamoros, Mexico; Maria Lucia Sciamarelli, **Cultura Inglesa**, Campinas, Brazil; Elisabete Thess, **Cultura Inglesa**, Petrópolis, Brazil; Catarina M. B. Pontes Kruppa, **Cultura Inglesa**, São Paulo, Brazil; Sheila Lima, **Curso Oxford**, Rio de Janeiro, Brazil; Elaine Florencio, Beth Vasconcelos, **English House Corporate**, Rio de Janeiro, Brazil; Vasti Rodrigues e Silva, **Fox Idiomas**, Rio de Janeiro, Brazil; Ricardo Ramos Miguel Cézar, Walter Júnior Ribeiro Silva, **Friends Language Center**, Itapaci, Brazil; Márcia Maria Pedrosa Sá Freire de Souza, **IBEU**, Rio de Janeiro, Brazil; Jerusa Rafael, **IBEUV**, Vitória, Brazil; Lilianne de Souza Oliveira, **ICBEU**, Manaus, Brazil; Liviane Santana Paulino de Carvalho, **ICBEU**, São Luís, Brazil; Manuel Marrufo Vásquez, **iempac Instituto de Enseñanza del Idioma Ingles**, Tequila, Mexico; Nora Aquino, **Instituto de Ciencias y Humanidades Tabasco**, Villahermosa, Mexico; Andrea Grimaldo, **Instituto Laurens**, Monterrey, Mexico; Cenk Aykut, Staci Jenkins, Kristen Okada, **Interactive College of Technology**, Chamblee, GA, USA; Imeen Manahan-Vasquez, Zuania Serrano, **Interactive Learning Systems**, Pasadena, TX, USA; Nicholas J. Jackson, **Jackson English School**, Uruapan, Mexico; Marc L. Cummings, **Jefferson Community and Technical College**, Louisville, KY, USA; Solange Nery Veloso, **Nery e Filho Idiomas**, Rio de Janeiro, Brazil; Tomas Sparano Martins, **Phil Young's English School**, Curitiba, Brazil; Paulo Cezar Lira Torres, **PRIME Language Center**, Vitória, Brazil; Angie Vasconcellos, **Robin English School**, Petrópolis, Brazil; Barbara Raifsnider, **San Diego Community College District**, San Diego, CA, USA; James Drury de Matos Fonseca, **SENAC**, Fortaleza, Brazil; Manoel Fialho da Silva Neto, **SENAC**, Recife, Brazil; Marilyn Ponder, **Tecnológico de Monterrey**, Irapuato, Mexico; Linda M. Holden, **The College of Lake County**, Grayslake, IL, USA; Janaína da Silva Cardoso, **UERJ**, Rio de Janeiro, Brazil; Gustavo Reges Ferreira, Sandlei Moraes de Oliveira, **UFES**, Vitória, Brazil; Nancy Alarcón Mendoza, **UNAM**, **Facultad de Estudios Superiores Zaragoza**, Mexico City, Mexico; Rosa Awilda López Fernández, **UNAPEC**, Santo Domingo, Dominican Republic; Vera Lúcia Ratide, **Unilínguas**, São Leopoldo, Brazil; Elsa Yolanda Cruz Maldonado, **Universidad Autónoma de Chiapas**, Tapachula, Mexico; Deida Perea, **Universidad Autónoma de Ciudad Juárez**, Ciudad Juárez, Mexico; Gabriela Ladrón de Guevara de León, **Universidad Autónoma de la Ciudad de México**, Mexico City, Mexico; Juan Manuel Ardila Prada, **Universidad Autónoma de Occidente**, Cali, Colombia; Lizzete G. Acosta Cruz, **Universidad Autónoma de Zacatecas**, Fresnillo, Mexico; Ary Guel, Fausto Noriega, Areli Martínez Suaste, **Universidad Autónoma de Zacatecas**, Zacatecas, Mexico; Gabriela Cortés Sánchez, **Universidad Autónoma Metropolitana Azcapotzalco**, Mexico City, Mexico; Secundino Isabeles Flores, Guillermo Guadalupe Duran Garcia, Maria Magdalena Cass Zubiria, **Universidad de Colima**, Colima, Mexico; Alejandro Rodríguez Sánchez, **Universidad del Golfo de México Norte**, Orizaba, Mexico; Fabiola Meneses Argüello, **Universidad La Salle Cancún**, Cancún, Mexico; Claudia Isabel Fierro Castillo, **Universidad Politécnica de Chiapas**, Tuxtla Gutierrez, Mexico; Eduardo Aguirre Rodríguez, M.A. Carolina Labastida Villa, **Universidad Politécnica de Quintana Roo**, Cancún, Mexico; Gabriela de Jesús Aubry González, **Universidad TecMilenio Campus Veracruz**, Boca del Rio, Mexico; Frank Ramírez Marín, **Universidad Veracruzana**, Boca del Río, Mexico.

Additional thanks are owed to Alex Tilbury for revising the Self-assessment charts, Paul MacIntyre for revising the Grammar Plus section, and Karen Kawaguchi for writing the Vocabulary Plus section.

Welcome to **Passages!**

Congratulations! You have learned the basics; now it's time to raise your English to a whole new level.

Your journey through each unit of ***Passages Third Edition*** will include a range of activities that will **progressively expand your language ability** in a variety of contexts, including formal and informal communication.

Along the way, you will encounter frequent communication reviews and progress checks that will **systematically consolidate your learning**, while **additional grammar and vocabulary practice** is available whenever you need it in the Grammar Plus and Vocabulary Plus sections in the back of this book.

RAISING YOUR ENGLISH TO A WHOLE NEW LEVEL

Unique features to boost your English proficiency!

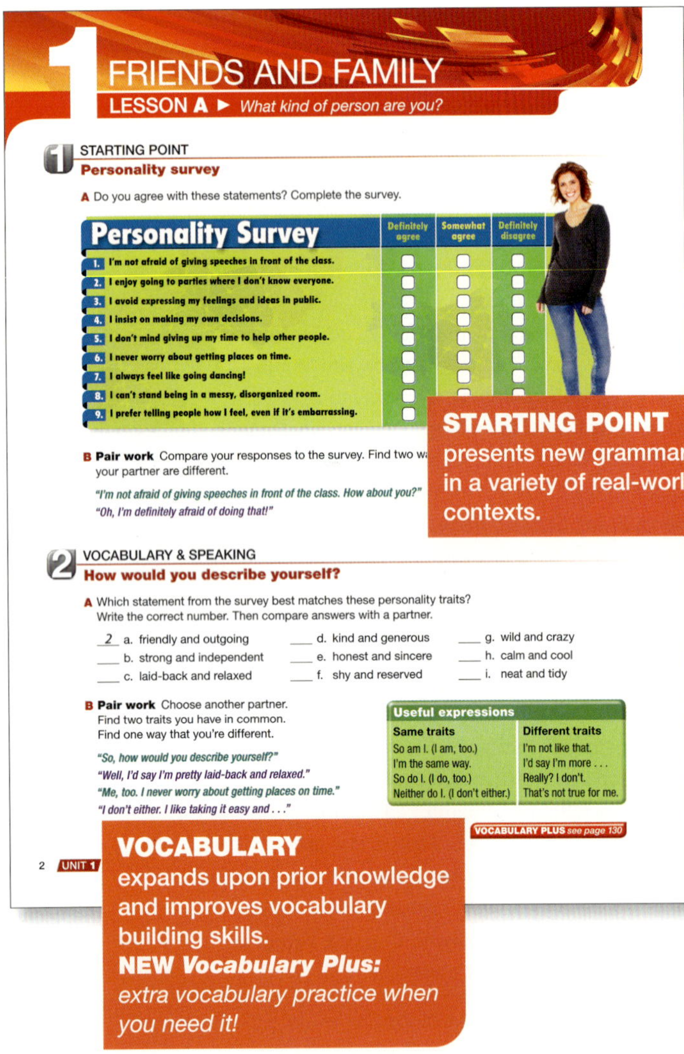

1 FRIENDS AND FAMILY

LESSON A ► *What kind of person are you?*

1 STARTING POINT
Personality survey

A Do you agree with these statements? Complete the survey.

Personality Survey

	Definitely agree	Somewhat agree	Definitely disagree
1. I'm not afraid of giving speeches in front of the class.	☐	☐	☐
2. I enjoy going to parties where I don't know everyone.	☐	☐	☐
3. I avoid expressing my feelings and ideas in public.	☐	☐	☐
4. I insist on making my own decisions.	☐	☐	☐
5. I don't mind giving up my time to help other people.	☐	☐	☐
6. I never worry about getting places on time.	☐	☐	☐
7. I always feel like going dancing!	☐	☐	☐
8. I can't stand being in a messy, disorganized room.	☐	☐	☐
9. I prefer telling people how I feel, even if it's embarrassing.	☐	☐	☐

B Pair work Compare your responses to the survey. Find two w... your partner are different.

"I'm not afraid of giving speeches in front of the class. How about you?"
"Oh, I'm definitely afraid of doing that!"

2 VOCABULARY & SPEAKING
How would you describe yourself?

A Which statement from the survey best matches these personality traits? Write the correct number. Then compare answers with a partner.

_2_ a. friendly and outgoing ___ d. kind and generous ___ g. wild and crazy
___ b. strong and independent ___ e. honest and sincere ___ h. calm and cool
___ c. laid-back and relaxed ___ f. shy and reserved ___ i. neat and tidy

B Pair work Choose another partner. Find two traits you have in common. Find one way that you're different.

"So, how would you describe yourself?"
"Well, I'd say I'm pretty laid-back and relaxed."
"Me, too. I never worry about getting places on time."
"I don't either. I like taking it easy and . . ."

Useful expressions

Same traits	Different traits
So am I. (I am, too.)	I'm not like that.
I'm the same way.	I'd say I'm more . . .
So do I. (I do, too.)	Really? I don't.
Neither do I. (I don't either.)	That's not true for me.

VOCABULARY PLUS *see page 130*

2 UNIT 1

STARTING POINT
presents new grammar in a variety of real-world contexts.

VOCABULARY
expands upon prior knowledge and improves vocabulary building skills.
NEW Vocabulary Plus:
extra vocabulary practice when you need it!

GRAMMAR
is explored in context and builds on previously encountered structures.
Grammar Plus:
extra grammar explanations and practice when you need it!

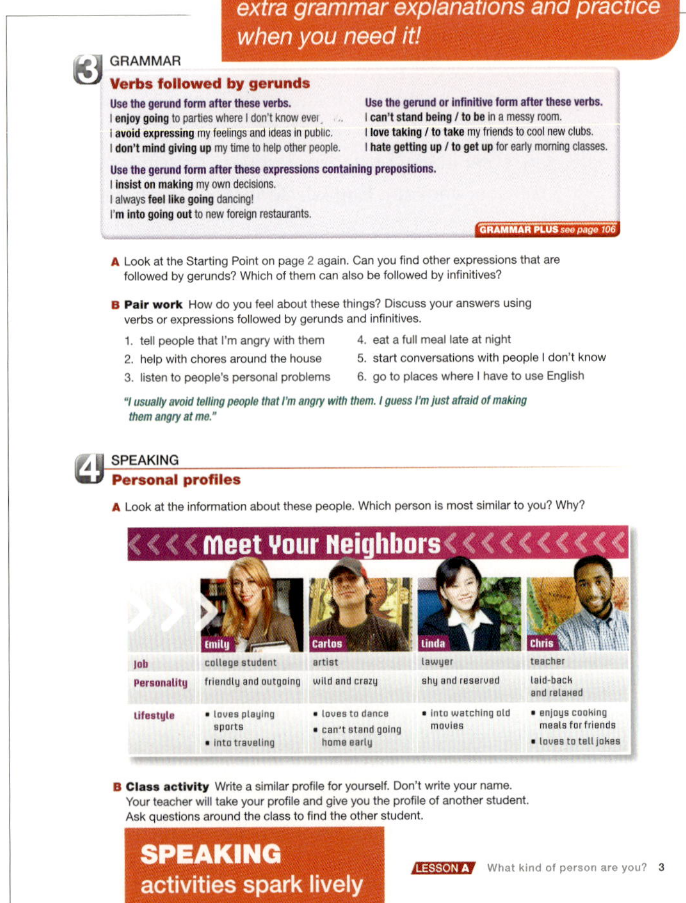

3 GRAMMAR
Verbs followed by gerunds

Use the gerund form after these verbs.
I **enjoy going** to parties where I don't know everyone.
I **avoid expressing** my feelings and ideas in public.
I **don't mind giving up** my time to help other people.

Use the gerund or infinitive form after these verbs.
I **can't stand being / to be** in a messy room.
I **love taking / to take** my friends to cool new clubs.
I **hate getting up / to get up** for early morning classes.

Use the gerund form after these expressions containing prepositions.
I **insist on making** my own decisions.
I always **feel like going** dancing!
I'm **into going out** to new foreign restaurants.

GRAMMAR PLUS *see page 106*

A Look at the Starting Point on page 2 again. Can you find other expressions that are followed by gerunds? Which of them can also be followed by infinitives?

B Pair work How do you feel about these things? Discuss your answers using verbs or expressions followed by gerunds and infinitives.

1. tell people that I'm angry with them
2. help with chores around the house
3. listen to people's personal problems
4. eat a full meal late at night
5. start conversations with people I don't know
6. go to places where I have to use English

"I usually avoid telling people that I'm angry with them. I guess I'm just afraid of making them angry at me."

4 SPEAKING
Personal profiles

A Look at the information about these people. Which person is most similar to you? Why?

Meet Your Neighbors

	Emily	Carlos	Linda	Chris
Job	college student	artist	lawyer	teacher
Personality	friendly and outgoing	wild and crazy	shy and reserved	laid-back and relaxed
Lifestyle	• loves playing sports • into traveling	• loves to dance • can't stand going home early	• into watching old movies	• enjoys cooking meals for friends • loves to tell jokes

B Class activity Write a similar profile for yourself. Don't write your name. Your teacher will take your profile and give you the profile of another student. Ask questions around the class to find the other student.

LESSON A What kind of person are you? 3

SPEAKING
activities spark lively discussions focusing on interesting and relevant situations.

5 LISTENING
Life in Sydney

A Listen to Maria and Ian talk about life in Sydney. Who seems to enjoy living there more?

B Listen again. Which person has these opinions? Choose Maria, Ian, or both.

	Maria	Ian	Both
1. It's easy to get around Sydney.	☐	☐	☐
2. The beaches are great.	☐	☐	☐
3. The rents are expensive.	☐	☐	☐
4. It's a fun place to live.	☐	☐	☐
5. The restaurants are all expensive.	☐	☐	☐
6. Life is better in a smaller town.	☐	☐	☐

LISTENING activities sharpen essential listening comprehension skills.

6 DISCUSSION
Quality of life

A Rate these quality-of-life issues as very important (2), important (1), or not important (0). Can you add one more to the list?

Quality of Life

- ___ affordable housing
- ___ a variety of restaurants
- ___ beautiful parks
- ___ convenient public transportation
- ___ exciting
- ___ first-clas
- ___ historic
- ___ low crim

B **Pair work** Which three issues are the most impor considering where to live? Explain why.

"I guess affordable housing and exciting nightlife are the m find a place I could afford that was near someplace fun."

"I know what you mean. But for me, I guess low crime rate I want to live somewhere where I feel safe. I don't mind if

C **Class activity** Share your answers with your clas mentioned most often?

24 UNIT 3 Exploring new cities

7 WRITING
Brainstorming

Brainstorming means making a list of ideas about a topic. Then you can use this list to come up with a topic sentence and ideas to support it.

A **Group work** Brainstorm as many ideas as you can to add to the dos and don'ts for living on a budget.

Living on a Tight Bu

Do	*Don't*
• *compare prices*	• *buy the f*
• *look for sales*	• *buy bran*
• *check ads for used items*	• *use cred*

B **Group work** Brainstorm dos and don'ts for one of

- getting over a bad cold
- staying safe in a bi

C Read this paragraph about living on a tight budget. T sentence and a similar paragraph about your topic u

Living on a tight budget is easy if you follow sor shopping. First of all, you should never buy somethi need to check at least a few other stores and go onl don't be in a hurry! If you take your time, you might now, ask a salesperson if there's going to be one so secondhand, items. You can check in the newspape for. Finally, you might get a better price at some sto credit card, so be sure to ask about cash discounts.

D **Pair work** Exchange brainstorming lists and parag Then answer the questions.

1. How many brainstorming ideas did your partner u chose the best ones?
2. Do you have any questions about your partner's p you disagree with?
3. Can you think of a good title for your partner's pa

WRITING tasks build academic writing skills through step-by-step activities.

Passages Third Edition is a two-level course that will open the door to communicating with greater fluency and proficiency, with:

- **more sophisticated** real-world grammar and vocabulary,
- **thought-provoking** discussions and academic writing activities,
- **more challenging** listening and reading comprehension topics.

READING passages drawn from authentic sources promote critical thinking and analysis.

7 READING
Cyber-begging

A **Pair work** Imagine that a stranger asked you for money to help pay off a frivolous debt. Would you help? Tell your partner. Then read the article.

Can you spare a dime for my Gucci bills?

There was a time when Karyn Bosnak couldn't pay a $59.00 bill at the grocery store. She was officially broke. She didn't have enough money to get on the subway, but she looked rich. She was a television producer, earned $900 a week, and had a closetful of designer labels like Gucci and Louis Vuitton. But she also had a $20,221.40 credit card bill and an empty bank account. Karyn decided that it was time for a change. She built a website and simply asked people to help her out by sending her a buck or two.

On the site, Karyn honestly explained her situation, Gucci shoes and all. "If 20,000 people gave me just $1, I'd be home free, and I'm sure there are 20,000 people out there who can afford to give me $1." Amazingly, it worked. Her website was visited by more than a million people. Although most donors just gave a few dollars, one generous donor sent $1,000. She was on TV and in newspapers and magazines. She was offered a book deal and a movie contract. And of course, she was able to pay off her credit card debt.

She also sold her designer clothes on eBay. In her closet, where the Gucci purses once sat, Karyn keeps all the letters that people have sent her. She's received teddy bears, subscriptions to *Vogue*, Dunkin' Donuts coupons, backpacks, jewelry, cat food, and candles.

It's hard to understand why so many people helped a total stranger pay off her huge credit card bill. Why did they do it? Karyn explains, "I was just honest about what happened; I didn't make up some sob story about saving the world." Her donors think it's funny and original, she argues, and view it less as a charity than as an entertainment site.

Imitators have sprung up all over the Internet, some with outrageously selfish requests like a BMW or a house. Actually, Karyn was not the first person to put up a website asking strangers for money. The practice has a name: "cyber-begging." Most sites receive little traffic and even less cash.

Karyn also had thousands of enemies and critics. People sent her hate mail and scolded her on websites. Karyn says she never let this anger bother her. "They are probably jealous they didn't think of it," she explains.

Source: "Brother, can you spare a dime for my Gucci bills?" by Janelle Brown, Salon.com

B Read the article again and answer the questions. Then compare your answers with a partner.

1. Why was Karyn in financial trouble?
2. What was her main solution to her problem? What else did she do?
3. Why did so many people respond positively to her website?

C **Group work** Discuss these questions. Then share your answers with the class.

1. Do you think Karyn was unethical, or was she simply clever?
2. What would you have done if you were Karyn?

LESSON B Information overload 61

KEEP MOVING UP!

More support is always available – when and where you need it!

The **WORKBOOK** provides extensive practice of grammar and vocabulary as well as additional reading and writing activities.

The **DIGITAL WORKBOOK** – a digital version of the Workbook – enables your teacher to provide instant feedback on your work.

AUDIO AND VIDEO on Cambridge One allows students to review on their own.

cambridgeone.org

Plan of **BOOK 1A**

	FUNCTIONS	GRAMMAR	VOCABULARY
UNIT 1 Friends and family pages 2–9			
A What kind of person are you? **B** Every family is different.	■ Describing personalities ■ Expressing likes and dislikes ■ Describing personal change ■ Stating advantages and disadvantages	■ Verbs followed by gerunds ■ Noun clauses after *be*	■ Personality collocations ■ Compound family terms
UNIT 2 Mistakes and mysteries pages 10–17			
A Life lessons **B** I can't explain it!	■ Describing rules and obligations in the past ■ Giving advice about the past ■ Speculating about past events ■ Offering explanations about past events	■ Past modals and phrasal modals of obligation ■ Modals with multiple uses	■ Collocations with *problem* ■ Verbs of belief
UNIT 3 Exploring new cities pages 18–25			
A Popular destinations **B** My kind of town	■ Describing and giving information about places ■ Stating preferences ■ Presenting contrasting information ■ Categorizing and evaluating issues	■ Defining and non-defining relative clauses ■ Order of modifiers ■ Connecting contrasting ideas	■ Features of cities ■ Compound terms for towns
UNITS 1–3 Communication review pages 26–27			
UNIT 4 Early birds and night owls pages 28–35			
A It's about time! **B** Tossing and turning	■ Describing routines and habits ■ Giving advice ■ Explaining reasons and conditions ■ Giving interpretations of meaning	■ Reduced time clauses ■ Clauses stating reasons and conditions	■ Phrasal verbs related to energy and sleep ■ Expressions related to sleep
UNIT 5 Communication pages 36–43			
A Making conversation **B** It's personal.	■ Describing types of conversationalists ■ Talking about appropriate behavior ■ Starting a conversation ■ Making small talk ■ Reporting what someone else has said	■ Infinitive and gerund phrases ■ Reported speech	■ Terms to describe behavior ■ Expressions for reported speech
UNIT 6 What's the real story? pages 44–51			
A That's some story! **B** Storytelling	■ Presenting information in chronological order ■ Narrating news events ■ Organizing and presenting information	■ Present perfect vs. simple past ■ Present perfect vs. present perfect continuous ■ Adverbs with the simple past and past perfect	■ News events ■ Storytelling expressions
UNITS 4–6 Communication review pages 52–53			
GRAMMAR PLUS: Additional grammar practice and explanation pages 106–117			
VOCABULARY PLUS: Additional vocabulary practice pages 130–135			

SPEAKING	LISTENING	WRITING	READING
■ Finding out what personality traits you have in common with your classmates ■ Comparing personal profiles ■ Talking about how you have changed or how you would like to change ■ Comparing families	■ Two people describe how they have changed ■ Two people compare similarities and differences between their families ■ A young man describes his recent family reunion	■ Identifying the topic sentence in a paragraph ■ Writing a paragraph about your most positive or negative quality	■ "From Circle of Friends to Modern Tribe": A group of friends can function as a family
■ Talking about past mistakes ■ Comparing reactions to a news story ■ Discussing what might have caused three mysterious events ■ Making guesses about unusual questions ■ Comparing opinions about a real-life unexplained event	■ A man talks about a bad decision he made ■ Three people talk about how they dealt with their problems ■ Two people talk about everyday mysteries	■ Brainstorming topic sentences and supporting ideas ■ Writing a paragraph with dos and don'ts	■ "Amnesia Spoils Newlyweds' Bliss": A man loses his memory after his wedding
■ Explaining why you'd like to visit a particular city ■ Choosing the right city for a particular purpose ■ Deciding which city is best to live in ■ Describing your hometown ■ Discussing quality-of-life issues	■ A TV show introduces two exciting cities ■ Two foreign students explain what they like about their host city ■ Two Sydney residents talk about the city	■ Organizing ideas with a mind map ■ Writing a paragraph about a place you know	■ "Rivals with a Lot in Common": The rivalry between two major Australian cities
■ Discussing personal energy levels ■ Talking about how to deal with stress ■ Giving advice on sleep and energy levels ■ Talking about sleeping habits ■ Interpreting dreams	■ Three people describe methods they use to lower stress ■ Two people describe their dreams and try to interpret them	■ Choosing the best topic sentence ■ Writing a paragraph giving advice on good habits	■ "To Sleep or Not to Sleep?": People are sleeping fewer hours than ever before
■ Discussing conversational styles ■ Discussing awkward social situations ■ Determining appropriate topics for small talk ■ Comparing who you confide in ■ Recounting an interesting conversation	■ People make small talk at parties ■ Two people tell some interesting news	■ Making an outline ■ Writing about a cultural rule	■ "Cell Phone Personality Types": What kind of cell phone user are you?
■ Determining if a story is true or false ■ Presenting a recent news story ■ Discussing how you follow the news ■ Telling stories about uncomfortable situations	■ A radio news broadcast ■ Two people describe complicated experiences ■ An actor describes some embarrassing moments	■ Putting events in chronological order ■ Writing a narrative paragraph	■ "It Happened to Me!": Two comical personal anecdotes

1 FRIENDS AND FAMILY

LESSON A ▶ *What kind of person are you?*

1 STARTING POINT
Personality survey

A Do you agree with these statements? Complete the survey.

Personality Survey	Definitely agree	Somewhat agree	Definitely disagree
1. I'm not afraid of giving speeches in front of the class.	☐	☐	☐
2. I enjoy going to parties where I don't know everyone.	☐	☐	☐
3. I avoid expressing my feelings and ideas in public.	☐	☐	☐
4. I insist on making my own decisions.	☐	☐	☐
5. I don't mind giving up my time to help other people.	☐	☐	☐
6. I never worry about getting places on time.	☐	☐	☐
7. I always feel like going dancing!	☐	☐	☐
8. I can't stand being in a messy, disorganized room.	☐	☐	☐
9. I prefer telling people how I feel, even if it's embarrassing.	☐	☐	☐

B Pair work Compare your responses to the survey. Find two ways you and your partner are different.

"I'm not afraid of giving speeches in front of the class. How about you?"
"Oh, I'm definitely afraid of doing that!"

2 VOCABULARY & SPEAKING
How would you describe yourself?

A Which statement from the survey best matches these personality traits? Write the correct number. Then compare answers with a partner.

_2_ a. friendly and outgoing
____ b. strong and independent
____ c. laid-back and relaxed
____ d. kind and generous
____ e. honest and sincere
____ f. shy and reserved
____ g. wild and crazy
____ h. calm and cool
____ i. neat and tidy

B Pair work Choose another partner. Find two traits you have in common. Find one way that you're different.

"So, how would you describe yourself?"
"Well, I'd say I'm pretty laid-back and relaxed."
"Me, too. I never worry about getting places on time."
"I don't either. I like taking it easy and . . ."

Useful expressions

Same traits	Different traits
So am I. (I am, too.)	I'm not like that.
I'm the same way.	I'd say I'm more . . .
So do I. (I do, too.)	Really? I don't.
Neither do I. (I don't either.)	That's not true for me.

VOCABULARY PLUS *see page 130*

3 GRAMMAR

Verbs followed by gerunds

Use the gerund form after these verbs.
I **enjoy going** to parties where I don't know everyone.
I **avoid expressing** my feelings and ideas in public.
I **don't mind giving up** my time to help other people.

Use the gerund or infinitive form after these verbs.
I **can't stand being / to be** in a messy room.
I **love taking / to take** my friends to cool new clubs.
I **hate getting up / to get up** for early morning classes.

Use the gerund form after these expressions containing prepositions.
I **insist on making** my own decisions.
I always **feel like going** dancing!
I'**m into going out** to new foreign restaurants.

GRAMMAR PLUS *see page 106*

A Look at the Starting Point on page 2 again. Can you find other expressions that are followed by gerunds? Which of them can also be followed by infinitives?

B Pair work How do you feel about these things? Discuss your answers using verbs or expressions followed by gerunds and infinitives.

1. tell people that I'm angry with them
2. help with chores around the house
3. listen to people's personal problems
4. eat a full meal late at night
5. start conversations with people I don't know
6. go to places where I have to use English

"I usually avoid telling people that I'm angry with them. I guess I'm just afraid of making them angry at me."

4 SPEAKING

Personal profiles

A Look at the information about these people. Which person is most similar to you? Why?

Meet Your Neighbors

	Emily	Carlos	Linda	Chris
Job	college student	artist	lawyer	teacher
Personality	friendly and outgoing	wild and crazy	shy and reserved	laid-back and relaxed
Lifestyle	• loves playing sports • into traveling	• loves to dance • can't stand going home early	• into watching old movies	• enjoys cooking meals for friends • loves to tell jokes

B Class activity Write a similar profile for yourself. Don't write your name. Your teacher will take your profile and give you the profile of another student. Ask questions around the class to find the other student.

5 LISTENING
Changes

A Listen to Marcos and Heather talk about how they have changed over the last five years. How did they change? Complete the chart with the expressions from the box.

kind and generous	friendly and outgoing	shy and reserved	wild and crazy

	used to be . . .	has become . . .
 Marcos		
 Heather		

B Listen again. Choose the person you think would be more likely to do each of these things this weekend.

	Marcos	Heather
1. stay out late at a big party	☐	☐
2. stay at home and watch TV	☐	☐
3. help someone with a personal problem	☐	☐
4. invite a friend to a funny movie	☐	☐

6 DISCUSSION
How have you changed?

A How have you changed over the last five years? What do you want to change now? Complete the chart.

	How I've changed	How I'd like to change
Habits		
Personality		
Likes and dislikes		

B Pair work Compare your charts. Ask follow-up questions.

"I used to watch a lot of TV, but now I don't."
"Really? What made you change?"
"Well, I was afraid of getting out of shape. So I . . ."

Useful expressions

Describing how you've changed	Describing how you'd like to change
I used to . . . , but now I . . .	I'd like to be more . . .
I think I've become more . . .	I'm interested in . . .

7 WRITING
Topic sentences

The main idea is usually found in the first sentence of the paragraph. This sentence is called the topic sentence.

A Read these paragraphs about people's best and worst qualities. Underline the topic sentence in each paragraph.

File Edit View Insert Format Tools Table Window Help

I think that my most positive quality is that I'm always pretty calm and cool, especially when something breaks. I'm really into solving tricky problems and finding solutions to things. My specialty is electronics. People come to me if something goes wrong with their computers or phones. For example, two days ago, my dad's brand new tablet suddenly froze up. He was afraid of causing more damage, so he asked me to figure out the problem. It only took me 15 minutes to fix it, and I loved doing it!

My most negative quality is that I'm not very neat and tidy. Sometimes I worry about being so disorganized, but I never feel like doing anything about it. My apartment is always a mess, so I can never find anything. Last week, for example, I finished doing some homework and then started to make dinner. In the morning, I couldn't find my assignment anywhere, so I had to redo it. I really want to change my bad habits, but I don't know where to start.

B Think about your own personal qualities. Make a list. Then decide which quality is the most positive and which is the most negative. Circle each one.

C Write a paragraph about either your most positive or your most negative quality. Make sure your paragraph has only one main idea.

D **Pair work** Exchange paragraphs with a partner. Then answer the questions.

1. What is your partner's topic sentence? Underline it.
2. What examples does your partner give to support the topic sentence?
3. What do you find most interesting about your partner's paragraph?

LESSON B ► *Every family is different.*

1 STARTING POINT
Different types of families

A Look at the families in the pictures. What's different about each type of family?

What's Your Family Like?

The Watsons, Sydney

"My wife and I both work now, and the extra money is great. The only trouble with being a **two-income family** is we don't spend as much time together."

The Wangs, Vancouver

"We're an **extended family** now that Grandma has moved in. The big advantage of having her at home is that she can babysit more often."

The Patels, London

"We're a typical **nuclear family** – it's just my sister, my parents, and me. The only bad thing about living in our house is there's only one bathroom!"

B Pair work What are some more advantages and disadvantages of each type of family in part A? Compare ideas.

"In a nuclear family, you might not see your grandparents every day. That's a disadvantage."

2 LISTENING & SPEAKING
How are their families different?

A Listen to Paul and Andrea talk about their families. What kind of family did each person grow up in? How have their families changed?

B Listen again. Match the people on the left with the phrases on the right.

1. Andrea *b*	a. has two daughters.
2. Andrea's husband ____	b. doesn't know her in-laws very well.
3. Andrea's sister-in-law ____	c. has three brothers.
4. Paul's sister ____	d. is looking forward to seeing the family.
5. Paul ____	e. will be cooking for 12 people.
6. Paul's mother ____	f. is a law student.

C Pair work Is your family similar to Paul's or Andrea's? How is it similar? How is it different?

3 GRAMMAR

Noun clauses after *be*

A noun clause is a part of a sentence with a subject and a predicate that functions as a noun. *That* is optional in noun clauses after *be*. Also notice the prepositions followed by gerunds in the first part of the sentences.

The only trouble **with** being a two-income family is **(that) we don't spend as much time together**.

The big advantage **of** having Grandma at home is **(that) she can babysit more often**.

GRAMMAR PLUS *see page 107*

A Look at the Starting Point on page 6 again. Can you find the noun clause in the last paragraph? Which preposition is used in the first part of the sentence?

B Combine the sentences. Then compare answers with a partner.

1. I'm the youngest in the family. The nice thing is I get a lot of attention.
   The nice thing about being the youngest in the family is that I get a lot of attention.
2. I have a younger sister. The trouble is she always wants to borrow my clothes.
3. I'm away at college. The bad part is that I miss my family.
4. I work at night. The worst thing is I can't have dinner with my family.
5. I'm the oldest in the family. One bad thing is that I always have to babysit.

C Complete the sentences with your own ideas. Then compare answers with a partner.

1. An advantage of being a twin is . . .
   that you always have someone to hang out with.
2. A problem with being an only child is . . .
3. One benefit of being the oldest is . . .
4. A big disadvantage of having an older sibling is . . .
5. The best thing about having a big family is . . .

4 DISCUSSION

Family matters

A Choose at least three questions you'd like to talk about with your group.

- ☐ What's the best thing about spending time with your family? What's the worst thing?
- ☐ What's one advantage of having a close family?
- ☐ What are some rules that people have to follow in your family?
- ☐ What's a benefit of having strict parents?
- ☐ Are you most likely to confide in a parent, a sibling, or a friend?
- ☐ Do you believe mothers and fathers should do the same chores?
- ☐ What are the advantages and disadvantages of having a two-income family?

B **Group work** Discuss the questions you chose in part A. Ask follow-up questions and make sure everyone in your group participates.

5 VOCABULARY
Compound family terms

A Match the family members on the left with the definitions on the right.

1. Your great-aunt is ____
2. Your granddaughter is ____
3. Your sister-in-law is ____
4. Your great-grandmother is ____

a. your father's or mother's grandmother.
b. your mother's or father's aunt.
c. your son's or daughter's daughter.
d. your wife's or husband's sister, or your brother's wife.

B Pair work Which of the family members in the box can be combined with a prefix or suffix in the chart? Complete the chart with a partner. What does each term mean?

aunt	daughter	mother	niece	son
brother	father	nephew	sister	uncle

great-	grand-	great-grand-	-in-law
aunt	*daughter*	*mother*	*sister*

"Your great-nephew is your brother's or sister's grandson."

VOCABULARY PLUS *see page 130*

6 LISTENING
Family reunion

A Listen to Victor tell a friend about his family reunion. What were they celebrating at the reunion?

B Listen again. In addition to Victor, who else was at the reunion? Select the people mentioned.

- ☐ 1. his grandfather
- ☐ 2. his uncle's cousin
- ☐ 3. his brother
- ☐ 4. his sister-in-law
- ☐ 5. his niece
- ☐ 6. his son
- ☐ 7. his mother-in-law
- ☐ 8. his cousin
- ☐ 9. friends of the family

7 READING

A family of friends

A Group work Do you tend to rely more on friends or family for help and advice? Why? Discuss with your group.

From Circle of Friends to Modern Tribe

Who celebrates birthdays and holidays with you? Who do you call when a crisis hits or when good luck strikes? If your answer is "my friends," you may have a "tribe."

When Ethan Watters took stock of his life a few years ago, the San Francisco writer realized that he was more dependent on friends than family, who lived hundreds of miles away.

"My friends were the centerpiece of my social life," he says. "They had taken on all the responsibilities that family members typically tackle – connecting me to the city, being a matchmaker, and helping me find jobs and places to live."

This circle of friends had become a tribe, which started when a group of artists, writers, and photographers began meeting for dinner every Tuesday night. Before long, they had begun functioning as a family of choice.

Watters grew to believe that non-family members forming close-knit social networks was a growing trend in the United States, and he wrote a book about it called *Urban Tribes: Are Friends the New Family?*

Modern tribes like Watters's often grow out of a shared interest or experience, but not every group of friends becomes a tribe.

The shift from "circle of friends" to tribe happens when members begin to treat each other like family – offering support without expectation of repayment; sheltering each other from gossip, stress, and attack; and looking out for everyone's overall well-being in life, work, and relationships.

Modern tribes often have a regular meeting place, annual parties, and group trips. Shared rites and rituals create a tribal story. "The members of the group may change," Watters says, "but the story of that group has central elements that remain. It gives the group a history."

Every tribe usually has an individual or core group that tends to its growth and survival. These tribal leaders are the ones who get everyone together on a regular basis and make the phone calls that get members excited about upcoming events.

Like families, tribes have a way of shaping their members: Individuals feel more confident, secure, loved, and stable. Even if your own family is close-knit, you may benefit from cultivating a family-like circle of friends. "The love and support we get from one," Watters says, "does not take away from the love and support we get from another."

Source: "My Tribe," by Erin Peterson, *Experience Life*

B Read the article and answer the questions. Then compare answers with a partner.

1. In what ways does Watters's circle of friends function as a family?
2. According to the article, what are some differences between a tribe and a family?
3. How does a group of friends become a tribe?

C Group work Discuss these questions. Then share your answers with the class.

1. What are some advantages and disadvantages of relying on friends for family-like support?
2. Do you consider yourself a member of a modern tribe? Why or why not?

2 MISTAKES AND MYSTERIES

LESSON A ▶ *Life lessons*

1 STARTING POINT

Learning the hard way

A Read about these people's problems. What mistake did each person make?

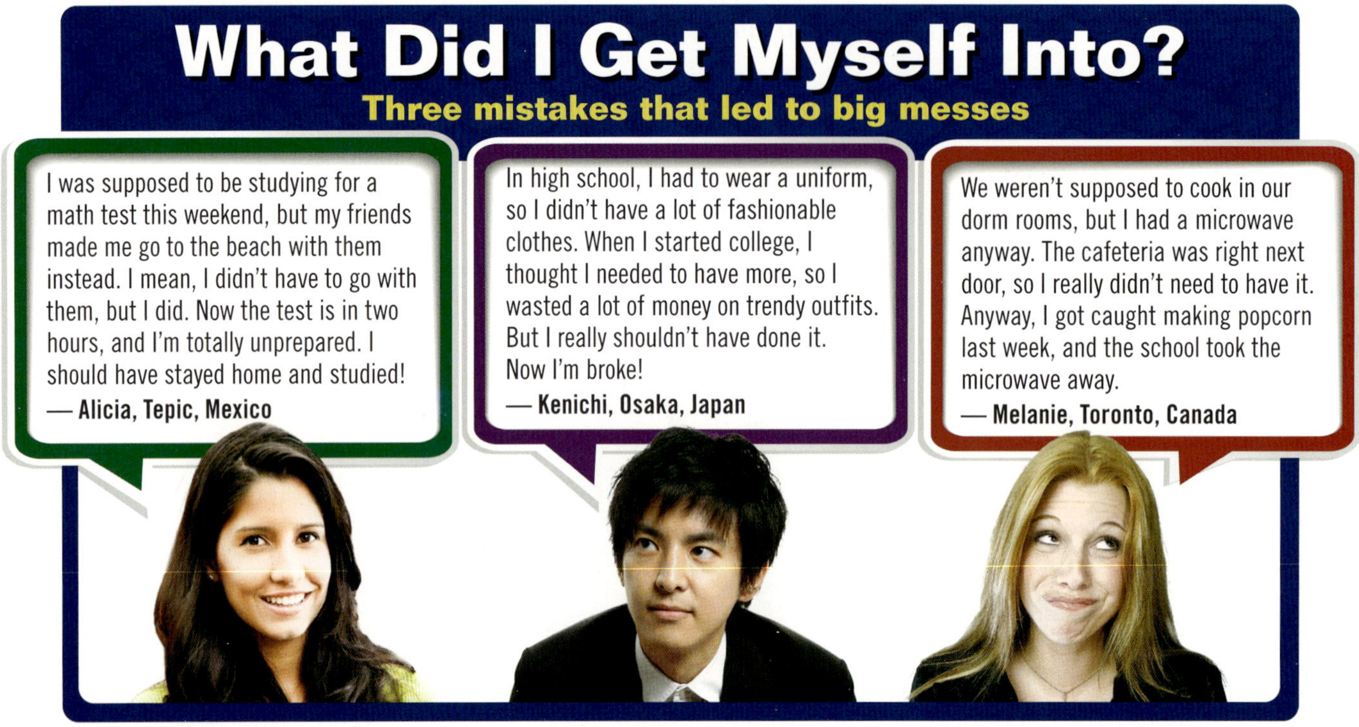

B Pair work What should each person do differently in the future? Compare ideas.

"I don't think Alicia should listen to her friends in the future."
"Yeah, I agree. She shouldn't let them influence her like that."

2 LISTENING

I'll never do that again!

A Listen to Frank talk about a bad decision he made. What was his decision? Why was it a bad one?

B Listen again. Are these statements true or false? Choose the correct answer.

	True	False
1. Frank and his neighbor were good friends.	☐	☐
2. Frank knew he was allergic to cats.	☐	☐
3. Frank marked his calendar to remember to feed the cat.	☐	☐
4. Frank forgot what time his train was going to leave.	☐	☐
5. Frank remembered to feed the cat on Saturday.	☐	☐

3 GRAMMAR

Past modals and phrasal modals of obligation

***Should have*, *was supposed to*, *had to*, and *needed to* all describe obligations in the past, although they have slightly different uses.**

I **should have** stayed home and studied! *(It was a good idea, but I didn't do it.)*
I **was supposed to** be studying this weekend. *(It was expected, but I didn't do it.)*
I **had to** wear a uniform. *(We were forced to do this.)*
I **didn't have to** go with my friends, but I did. *(There was no obligation.)*
I thought I **needed to** have more clothes. *(I thought this was necessary.)*

GRAMMAR PLUS *see page 108*

A Look at the Starting Point on page 10 again. Can you find other examples of past modals and phrasal modals of obligation? What does each one mean?

B Choose the answer that is true for each sentence. Then compare answers with a partner.

1. I shouldn't have invited them.
   - ☐ a. I didn't invite them.
   - ☐ b. I invited them.
2. That was a secret! You weren't supposed to tell anyone!
   - ☐ a. You didn't tell anyone.
   - ☐ b. You told someone.
3. We didn't have to study for the test.
   - ☐ a. We forgot to study.
   - ☐ b. We were prepared for the test.
4. I know Jane didn't like my cooking, but she didn't need to be so rude about it.
   - ☐ a. Jane was rude to me.
   - ☐ b. Jane wasn't rude to me.

C Complete the sentences with information about yourself. Then compare answers with a partner.

1. After I started high school, I had to . . .
   study a lot harder.
2. I made someone angry once because I wasn't supposed to . . .
3. I wasted a lot of money once because I thought I needed to . . .
4. When I had the opportunity, I should have . . .

4 DISCUSSION

Past experiences

A Look at the survey and choose the items that are true for you.

Have you ever . . .

- ☐ enjoyed doing something you weren't supposed to do?
- ☐ not done something you should have done?
- ☐ done something foolish that you didn't need to do?
- ☐ had to follow a rule you didn't like?
- ☐ had to enforce a rule you didn't like?

B Pair work Discuss your answers. Ask follow-up questions.

"Have you ever enjoyed doing something you weren't supposed to do?"
"Sure. At my old job, I wasn't supposed to take a long lunch, but I took long lunches at the park, anyway. How about you?"

5 VOCABULARY
Recognizing problems

A These verbs are often used to talk about problems. Use the verbs to replace the boldfaced words and phrases in the sentences.

aggravate avoid cause deal with identify ignore run into solve	a problem

1. My friend **never does anything about** his problems.
   My friend always ignores his problems.
2. Maria can look at a broken bicycle and **find** the problem right away.
3. My sister is never afraid to **try to take care of** a difficult problem.
4. Dan always **makes** his problems **worse**.
5. Ruby always follows the recipe closely to **prevent** problems when she cooks.
6. Michael always **unexpectedly encounters** problems when he tries to fix things.
7. Carla is great at **completely fixing** any kind of problem at work.
8. Al is the kind of student who always **makes** problems for teachers.

B Pair work Tell your partner about people you know who are similar to the people in the sentences in part A.

"My cousin always ignores her problems. Her car is always making strange noises, but she never does anything about it."

VOCABULARY PLUS *see page 131*

6 LISTENING
Dealing with problems

A Listen to Ray (*R*), Felipe (*F*), and Jennifer (*J*) talk about a problem that they each had. What did each person finally do about the problem? Write the correct letter.

____ ignored it ____ dealt with it ____ aggravated it

B Listen again. Briefly describe each person's problem.

Ray: ______________________________

Felipe: ______________________________

Jennifer: ______________________________

7 WRITING
Brainstorming

Brainstorming **means making a list of ideas about a topic. Then you can use this list to come up with a topic sentence and ideas to support it.**

A Group work Brainstorm as many ideas as you can to add to the dos and don'ts for living on a budget.

Living on a Tight Budget

Do	*Don't*
• *compare prices*	• *buy the first thing you see*
• *look for sales*	• *buy brand names*
• *check ads for used items*	• *use credit cards*

B Group work Brainstorm dos and don'ts for one of these topics. Write your ideas.

- getting over a bad cold
- staying safe in a big city
- preparing for entrance exams

C Read this paragraph about living on a tight budget. Then write a topic sentence and a similar paragraph about your topic using your ideas.

Living on a tight budget is easy if you follow some simple rules when you go shopping. First of all, you should never buy something at the first store you visit. You need to check at least a few other stores and go online to compare prices. Second, don't be in a hurry! If you take your time, you might find a sale. If there are no sales right now, ask a salesperson if there's going to be one soon. Third, consider buying used, or secondhand, items. You can check in the newspaper or online to find what you're looking for. Finally, you might get a better price at some stores by paying cash instead of using a credit card, so be sure to ask about cash discounts.

D Pair work Exchange brainstorming lists and paragraphs with a partner. Then answer the questions.

1. How many brainstorming ideas did your partner use? Do you think he or she chose the best ones?
2. Do you have any questions about your partner's paragraph? Is there anything you disagree with?
3. Can you think of a good title for your partner's paragraph? Explain your choice.

1 STARTING POINT
A mysterious artist

A Read the article and the comments on the right. Whose comments do you agree with?

The Mystery of BANKSY

Banksy is a British graffiti artist who has become famous around the world for two things: his controversial work and the mystery surrounding him. Usually working in disguise or at night, Banksy has managed to keep his identity secret and both his fans and detractors alert. Any clues to his identity always make the news.

In 2010, *Time* magazine featured Banksy as one of the 100 most influential people of the year. Readers hoping to finally see his face must have been pretty disappointed when they saw the picture of Banksy – with a paper bag over his head.

In 2011, when a movie by Banksy was nominated for an Oscar, his graffiti appeared on buildings and signs around Los Angeles. (People thought he could have been trying to get publicity for the movie.) At that time, a passerby photographed a man busy taking photos of the graffiti. It may have been Banksy documenting his own work, but nobody is sure.

In 2013, a website claimed Banksy had been arrested and his identity finally revealed. However, the claims were later discovered to be false. It's not clear who was behind the hoax, but one thing was certain: Banksy's secret was still safe.

Reader Comments

CafeLife: People should stop trying to find out who Banksy is. It's a waste of time.

Hye_Jung: The magazine readers shouldn't have expected Banksy to reveal his identity just because of an article.

Paul2001: I'm certain Banksy must have wanted to win that Oscar. But would he have shown his face at the award ceremony?

ArtFan: Banksy does return to photograph his art, so it might have been him taking the pictures. He should be more careful.

Zorro565: Banksy shouldn't have painted on other people's property. That's illegal.

WebWatcher: That website hoax might have been planned by Banksy himself. What a joke.

More >>

B Pair work Compare your reactions to the article.

"The people who worked on his movie might know who Banksy is."

"Well, maybe, but I'm sure his family must know he is the mysterious artist."

2 GRAMMAR

Modals with multiple uses

To express degrees of certainty, use *must (not)*, *can't*, *could (not)*, *might (not)*, or *may (not)*.

I'm certain Banksy **must have wanted** to win that Oscar.
People thought he **could have been trying** to get publicity for the movie.
That website hoax **might have been planned** by Banksy himself.

To express obligation, advice, or opinions, use *should (not)*. Do not use *must (not) have* for obligations, advice, or opinions about the past.

Banksy **shouldn't have painted** on other people's property. *(obligation)*
He **should be** more careful. *(advice)*
The magazine readers **shouldn't have expected** Banksy to reveal his identity just because of an article. *(opinion)*

Also notice how these modals are used in the passive and continuous.

GRAMMAR PLUS *see page 109*

A Look at the Starting Point on page 14 again. What does each modal express? Which one is used in the passive?

B Use modals to write reactions to these situations. Then compare answers with a partner.

1. You and your friend planned to meet, but your friend never arrived.
   He might have been busy at work, but he should have called to tell me.
2. You loaned your classmate a lot of money last week, but she still hasn't repaid you.
3. You feel sick after a big fish dinner.
4. You receive flowers from a secret admirer.
5. You haven't received any phone calls or text messages in a week.
6. Your boss promised to promote you, but it still hasn't happened.

3 DISCUSSION

What's the explanation?

A Read these headlines about strange events. How would you explain them?

MYSTERY SOUND IRRITATES VILLAGE

Each night from midnight to 4 A.M., a mysterious humming sound keeps the 300 residents of Woodland, England, awake. There are no factories or large roads nearby, and so far nobody can explain the sound.

Colored Honey Puzzles Farmers

In a French region famous for its honey, bees have been producing it in shades of blue and green. Farmers say the honey is unsellable, and they are investigating the cause.

River Runs Red

Shocked residents watched in disbelief last week as the river running through their city turned a deep red color. Some people rushed to save a bottle of the colored water while they had the chance.

B Group work Discuss your explanations. Do you agree?

"Airplanes flying overhead could have caused the noise in that village."
"I'm not so sure. I think someone may have been making the sound on purpose as a prank."

Useful expressions

Disagreeing
I don't know.
I'm not so sure.
Well, maybe, but . . .
I know what you mean, but . . .

4 VOCABULARY & SPEAKING
Verbs of belief

A Put these verbs of belief in the correct columns. Discuss your answers with a partner.

assume	be positive	bet	figure	have a hunch	suppose
be certain	be sure	doubt	guess	know for a fact	suspect

Certain	Not certain
	assume

B Group work Use the verbs of belief to discuss these questions.

1. Why do giraffes have long necks?
2. Why do some buildings not have a thirteenth floor?
3. Is there life on other planets?
4. Why doesn't a haircut hurt?
5. Why do some people fall in love at first sight?
6. What color is an insect's blood?

"Why do giraffes have long necks?"
"I'm not sure, but I assume they have long necks to eat the leaves at the tops of trees."
"Yeah, I bet that's the reason why."

VOCABULARY PLUS *see page 131*

5 LISTENING & SPEAKING
Solving mysteries

A Listen to Sheila and Adam discussing some myths and mysteries researched by the TV show *Solving Mysteries*. Choose the ones discovered to be true.

☐ 1. Using a cell phone can cause a fire at a gas station.
☐ 2. Talking to plants for a short time will help them grow better.
☐ 3. A person can break a glass using just his or her voice.
☐ 4. Yawning is contagious.

B Listen again. What ideas did Sheila and Adam originally have? Answer the questions.

1. How did Sheila think that cell phones could cause fires?
____
2. Why did Adam doubt that talking to plants could help them grow?
____
3. Why did Sheila have trouble believing voices could break a glass?
____
4. Why didn't Adam believe that yawning could be contagious?
____

C Group work Brainstorm other mysteries you might like to have *Solving Mysteries* investigate for you. Can anyone in the group explain the mysteries?

6 READING
Do I know you?

A Group work What does *amnesia* mean? What are some things that might cause amnesia? Discuss with your group.

Amnesia Spoils Newlyweds' Bliss

What if the person you married forgot who you were? For one Texas couple, marriage became a blind date when the groom came down with amnesia days after their wedding.

Amy and Sean McNulty's wedding day started well, but ended with a shock. One of Sean's good friends was in a serious car accident after the wedding and ended up in a coma. Nevertheless, Amy and Sean decided to make their honeymoon trip according to plans.

At the airport, Sean realized he'd left his wallet in their car. He said to Amy, "I'll be right back." But he didn't return.

Amy contacted the police, who found Sean wandering near a motel three days later. He was confused and covered in bug bites. He had no idea who he was or who Amy was. Sean could not remember any personal details from his life, not even his mother.

Amy was now married to a man who viewed her as a stranger. "I wondered, you know, is he going to remember me? How is our relationship going to, you know, form?" said Amy.

This was a big change after a six-year courtship and plenty of shared memories.

When Sean got out of the hospital, Amy had to give him a tour of their home. Although he had a room devoted to music, he couldn't even remember what it meant to hear music.

Psychiatrist Dr. Daniel Brown says Sean's amnesia might have been caused by a series of stressful moments, like his friend's car accident. According to Dr. Brown, Sean's brain didn't connect with his identity anymore. "He doesn't know who Sean McNulty is and has no personal memories or autobiographical memories to account for who he might be."

Dr. Brown explained that amnesia was like forgetting the name of a file you stored on your computer. "You know it's there but you can't find it," said Brown. "His memory is like that. He still has the file."

Fortunately, better times soon arrived. The day before their first anniversary, Sean's memories flooded back in an instant. He soon remembered everything, including their wedding. "I remember shoving cake in her face," said Sean. "It was great."

Sean views the experience as a chance to confirm he picked the right bride. "I got to see how much she loves me," said Sean. "We have a much stronger and closer bond from the experience. I couldn't have found a better woman to spend my life with."

Source: "Amnesia Spoils Newlyweds' Bliss," *ABC News*

B Read the article. Are these statements true or false? Choose the correct answer.

	True	False
1. Sean's amnesia began after he was in a car accident.	☐	☐
2. Sean and Amy didn't know each other well before they got married.	☐	☐
3. Sean shoved cake in Amy's face when he remembered who she was.	☐	☐
4. The amnesia might have been caused by stress.	☐	☐

C Group work Discuss these questions. Then share your answers with the class.

1. What would you have done if you had been in Amy's position?
2. What would be some of the problems you'd face if you ever forgot everything?

3 EXPLORING NEW CITIES

LESSON A ▶ *Popular destinations*

1 STARTING POINT
Cities of the world

A Read about these cities. Which city would you most like to visit?

BARCELONA

Barcelona is famous for museums, nightlife, and seafood – and for the architect Antoni Gaudí, who designed several of the city's most distinctive buildings. Most restaurants here stay open until midnight, when many locals are still enjoying dinner.

BEIJING

Beijing has many popular tourist attractions, which include the Summer Palace and the Forbidden City. Tourists who come here for the first time are amazed by the crowds, the busy streets, and the constantly changing skyline.

SEOUL

Seoul is well known for its spicy food and its shopping areas, where you can find everything from antique pottery to custom-made clothing. The Myeong-dong area has dozens of shops that sell the latest fashions.

SYDNEY

The place where most tourists go first in Sydney is the famous Opera House, but this Australian city also has great restaurants and museums. The spring and fall are the seasons when most people come to visit.

B Pair work Tell your partner about a city you know.

"I know Vancouver. It's got the ocean on one side and mountains on the other. It's really beautiful, but it's expensive . . . "

2 LISTENING
Where in the world . . . ?

A Listen to Diana and Matt talk about two cities. Who is talking about Athens and who is talking about Seoul?

B Listen again. Who mentions these topics, Diana (*D*) or Matt (*M*)? Write the correct letter.

____ 1. founded 3,000 years ago	____ 4. a river	____ 7. traffic
____ 2. delicious spicy food	____ 5. a subway system	____ 8. street vendors
____ 3. beautiful beaches	____ 6. monuments	____ 9. nightlife

3 GRAMMAR

Defining and non-defining relative clauses

A defining relative clause defines or gives essential information about a noun.
The Myeong-dong area has dozens of shops **that sell the latest fashions**.
The spring and fall are the seasons **when most people come to visit**.

A non-defining relative clause gives optional information about a noun and cannot begin with the pronoun *that*. Notice the use of commas.
Most restaurants here stay open until midnight, **when many locals are still enjoying dinner**.
Beijing has many popular tourist attractions, **which include the Summer Palace and the Forbidden City**.

GRAMMAR PLUS *see page 110*

A Look at the Starting Point on page 18 again. Can you find more relative clauses?

B Underline the relative clauses in the sentences and add commas where necessary. Write *D* for a defining and *ND* for a non-defining relative clause.

ND 1. Bangkok, which is the capital of Thailand, has many excellent restaurants and markets.
____ 2. Over one million people come to Pamplona in July when the festival of San Fermín takes place in this Spanish city.
____ 3. Aden is an ancient port city that is located in southern Yemen.
____ 4. Bogotá which is situated on a high plateau in central Colombia has frequently changing weather.
____ 5. Montreal is a sophisticated city where some of the best cuisine in Canada is found.
____ 6. São Paulo which is the biggest city in Brazil is one of the world's most populated cities.

C Join the sentences using non-defining relative clauses. Then compare answers.

1. Gaudí designed Barcelona's Park Güell. You can see fabulous sculptures there.
2. Seoul's name comes from the ancient word *seorabeol*. *Seorabeol* means "capital."
3. The center of Beijing is Tiananmen Square. It is the world's largest public square.
4. A great time to visit Seoul is in the fall. This is when Koreans celebrate the Chuseok festival.
5. Fast-food restaurants are already fairly common in China. They are increasing in number each year.
6. Australia's first European settlers came to Sydney in the late 1700s. They were originally from Great Britain.

4 SPEAKING

A great place to visit

A Which of the cities on page 18 would you like to visit? Write three sentences explaining your reasons. Use relative clauses where appropriate.

Barcelona is a city that I'd like to visit because . . .

B **Pair work** Tell your partner which city you'd like to visit and why.

5 VOCABULARY
What makes a city?

A Are these features of cities more important to tourists or to residents? Put the words in the correct columns. Add ideas of your own.

climate	crime rate	green spaces	job market	neighborhoods	shopping
cost of living	cuisine	hotels	landmarks	nightlife	transportation system

Important to tourists	Important to residents	Important to both

B Pair work Use the features from part A to talk about your city. Give examples and add extra information.

"Salvador is famous all over Brazil for its cuisine. Acarajé is one of the most popular foods, and it's really delicious. It's a deep-fried cake that's made from mashed beans."

VOCABULARY PLUS *see page 132*

6 LISTENING
What's the city like?

A Listen to Carlos and Vicki talk about San Francisco. Who seems to like the city better?

B Listen again. Choose the city features that Carlos and Vicki mention.

☐ 1. climate ☐ 3. shopping ☐ 5. hotels ☐ 7. landmarks ☐ 9. cuisine
☐ 2. architecture ☐ 4. customs ☐ 6. job market ☐ 8. nightlife

7 DISCUSSION
Perfect places

A Answer the questions with your own ideas.

What is...

1. a good city for budget travelers? ______________________
2. a good city for a honeymoon? ______________________
3. a place that would make a great family vacation spot? ______________________
4. a city where you'd like to live for a few years? ______________________
5. a good city to go to school in? ______________________
6. a place that you would never want to visit? ______________________

B Pair work Discuss your answers.

"I think New York is a good place for budget travelers."
"I'm not sure I agree. New York is incredibly expensive."
"That's true, but there are lots of cheap fast-food restaurants . . ."

Useful expressions

Agreeing with an opinion	Disagreeing with an opinion
I think you're right.	I'm not sure I agree.
I'm with you.	Maybe, but don't you think . . . ?
That's true.	Really?
I think so, too.	I know what you mean, but . . .

C Group work Join another pair and try to agree on one answer for each question.

8 WRITING
Organizing ideas with a mind map

Making a mind map is a good way of organizing your brainstorming ideas. Mind maps help you map out the supporting details about your topic.

A Look at the phrases in the box about Cuzco, Peru. Choose the main idea and write it in the center of the mind map. Then write the supporting details around it.

a mix of history and culture	great shopping	something for everyone
beautiful architecture	nice hotels	wonderful restaurants

B Read the paragraph about Cuzco. Underline the ideas from the mind map in the paragraph.

Cuzco has something for everyone. It's one of the oldest cities in the Americas, and it was once the capital of the Inca empire. Today, Cuzco is Peru's tourist capital because of its unique mix of history and culture. People who are interested in architecture will love the nearby Inca ruins of Machu Picchu and the palace of Inca Roca. Cuzco has many places to stay, which range from first-class hotels to cozy inns. There are also many cafés and restaurants where you can eat delicious local dishes or international cuisine. Also, Cuzco has great markets where you can shop for local arts and crafts. When you visit Cuzco, you should try to experience all it has to offer.

C Choose a place you know and make your own mind map. Be sure the main idea is general and the map contains several supporting ideas.

D Write a paragraph based on the ideas in your mind map.

E **Pair work** Exchange paragraphs with a partner. Then answer the questions.

1. Are there enough supporting details? Are there any details you'd like your partner to add?
2. Does the content of the paragraph reflect the ideas in the mind map?
3. Would you like to visit the place your partner wrote about? Why or why not?

LESSON B ▶ *My kind of town*

1 STARTING POINT
City search

A Complete the descriptions with the sentences below. Then compare answers.

This exciting large city with bustling streets is a great place to live. Most evenings you can choose from a movie, a concert, or even a museum. (1) ____ There are lots of jobs here, and the average salary is about $4,000 per month. (2) ____ Our efficient new subway system can get you anywhere you want to go. (3) ____

This is a picturesque little resort town with year-round outdoor activities. There's something to do in all four seasons. But there's not much action here at night. (4) ____ There are many quaint little stores and boutiques in this beautiful town. (5) ____ Apartments are affordable, too. You can get a great place for about $1,000 a month, and average monthly salaries are about $2,500. (6) ____

a. However, housing costs are high. A nice apartment is about $2,500 per month.
b. So, even though our streets are safe, the evenings can be dull.
c. But be careful – in spite of all the late-night activity, the crime rate is high.
d. On the other hand, it can sometimes be difficult to find a job.
e. Although it's fast, clean, and cheap, it's pretty crowded during rush hour. Nevertheless, it's becoming one of the most popular ways for people to get to work.
f. Despite the attractive location, the prices of houses are surprisingly reasonable.

B Pair work Which place do you think has more to offer – the city or the town?

2 VOCABULARY
Compound terms for towns

A These compound terms describe different types of towns. How would you define each one?

border town	college town	mountain town	resort town	suburban town
coastal town	industrial town	port town	rural town	tourist town

A border town is near a border with another state or country.

B Pair work Which of the terms best describes your hometown? Which best describes the town where you'd like to live someday? Compare ideas.

VOCABULARY PLUS *see page 132*

3 GRAMMAR

Order of modifiers

When two or more modifiers occur in a sentence, they usually follow this order.

	Quality	Size	Age	Type	Noun	Descriptive phrase
this	exciting	large			city	with bustling streets
a	picturesque	little		resort	town	with year-round outdoor activities
a	run-down		old	port	town	that has seen better days

GRAMMAR PLUS *see page 111*

A Look at the Starting Point on page 22 again. Can you find more sentences that have two or more modifiers?

B Write descriptions of places you know. Then compare answers with a partner.

1. a nearby city or town that you frequently visit
   Middleton is a typical suburban town with a good shopping mall.
2. a place you'd like to visit one day
3. a place tourists to your country want to see
4. a place you enjoy visiting, but wouldn't want to live in

4 GRAMMAR

Connecting contrasting ideas

You can use these words and phrases to connect contrasting ideas.

despite	although	however	on the other hand
in spite of	even though	nevertheless	

GRAMMAR PLUS *see page 111*

A Look at the Starting Point on page 22 again. What words and phrases connect the contrasting ideas?

B Choose the words that are true for you. Then complete the sentences.

1. Although I (*would*) / *wouldn't* like to live in this town forever, . . .
   Although I would like to live in this town forever, I'll have to move if rents go up.
2. There are *not many* / *a lot of* things I like about this town. However, . . .
3. Even though finding an apartment is *easy* / *difficult* in this town, . . .
4. Despite the high cost of living in this city, there are *a number of* / *no* . . .
5. The *spring* / *summer* / *fall* / *winter* here is very nice. On the other hand, . . .
6. Most places in this town close *early* / *late*. In spite of that, . . .
7. The areas around this town are mainly *rural* / *suburban* / *urban*. Nevertheless, . . .

C Pair work Discuss your answers. Ask and answer follow-up questions.

"Although I'd like to live in this town forever, I'll have to move if rents go up."
"Really? Where would you move?"
"I'm not sure. I hope someplace cheaper, but still near here."

5 LISTENING
Life in Sydney

A Listen to Maria and Ian talk about life in Sydney. Who seems to enjoy living there more?

B Listen again. Which person has these opinions? Choose Maria, Ian, or both.

	Maria	Ian	Both
1. It's easy to get around Sydney.	☐	☐	☐
2. The beaches are great.	☐	☐	☐
3. The rents are expensive.	☐	☐	☐
4. It's a fun place to live.	☐	☐	☐
5. The restaurants are all expensive.	☐	☐	☐
6. Life is better in a smaller town.	☐	☐	☐

6 DISCUSSION
Quality of life

A Rate these quality-of-life issues as very important (2), important (1), or not important (0). Can you add one more to the list?

Quality of Life

____ affordable housing	____ exciting nightlife	____ pleasant weather
____ a variety of restaurants	____ first-class health care	____ varied retail shops
____ beautiful parks	____ historic neighborhoods	____ wireless hot spots
____ convenient public transportation	____ low crime rates	____ ______________

B Pair work Which three issues are the most important to you personally when considering where to live? Explain why.

"I guess affordable housing and exciting nightlife are the most important to me. I'd love to find a place I could afford that was near someplace fun."

"I know what you mean. But for me, I guess low crime rates are probably the most important. I want to live somewhere where I feel safe. I don't mind if it's a little boring."

C Class activity Share your answers with your classmates. Which issues were mentioned most often?

7 READING
Melbourne versus Sydney

A Pair work What do you know about the Australian cities of Melbourne and Sydney? Tell your partner. Then read the article.

RIVALS with a lot IN COMMON

What's the truth behind the rivalry between **Melbourne** and **Sydney?**

According to Melbournians, they live in a paradise where ideas are discussed, the arts are celebrated, and life is beautiful. Sydneysiders claim to live in the same kind of place – only better. Nobody can agree on how the rivalry between Sydney and Melbourne started, but it's been going on for as long as anyone can remember.

If you believe the stereotypes that fuel this rivalry, Melbourne is just a quaint coastal city with nothing to do unless you're into indie music festivals and a slow-paced lifestyle, while Sydney is an expensive, unfriendly place with a focus on business and no place to park. If you believe what Melbournians and Sydneysiders say, the cities don't have much in common except that they're both Australian cities whose residents love where they live.

In reality, Sydney is a warm, beautiful city with lots of green, cross-harbor ferries, and world-class beaches, while Melbourne's right-in-the-city beaches are near colorful neighborhoods where there are plenty of things to do for entertainment.

Both Melbourne and Sydney have fabulous restaurants featuring cuisine from just about anywhere in the world, and both offer nightlife possibilities with something for everyone. In addition, both cities feature a year-round schedule of art and music festivals, as well as other cultural events catering to every taste. And their excellent public transportation systems help you get around easily.

It's true that Melbourne tends to have less rain than Sydney and that Sydney's average temperatures are higher, but it's wonderfully pleasant in either place. And while the cost-of-living is a little lower in Melbourne and salaries are higher in Sydney, prices in both really are quite comparable.

So, what's the rivalry all about? It probably comes down to civic pride. Residents of both of these world-class cities are rightly proud of where they live, and though there are differences, the differences are not really all that extreme. If you're not convinced, visit both and see for yourself.

Melbourne

Sydney

B Read the article again. Are these statements true (*T*), false (*F*), or is the information not given (*NG*) in the article? Write the correct letters.

____ 1. The rivalry between Sydney and Melbourne is a recent development.
____ 2. Life in Sydney, like in Melbourne, can also be slow.
____ 3. It's hard to get anywhere in Melbourne or Sydney without a car.
____ 4. It costs slightly less to live in Melbourne than it does in Sydney.

C Group work Discuss these questions. Then share your answers with the class.

1. Why do you think people in Melbourne and Sydney tend to focus on the differences between the two cities rather than on the similarities?
2. Are there any cities in your country that have a rivalry? How are the cities similar and different? Is the rivalry based on stereotypes or on facts?

COMMUNICATION REVIEW

UNITS 1–3

SELF-ASSESSMENT

How well can you do these things? Choose the best answer.

I can . . .	Very well	OK	A little
▶ Express personal likes and dislikes and give relevant explanations (Ex. 1)	☐	☐	☐
▶ Make and evaluate recommendations to improve a city in a problem-solving discussion (Ex. 2)	☐	☐	☐
▶ Understand anecdotes and say how the speakers feel about past mistakes (Ex. 3)	☐	☐	☐
▶ Describe past mistakes in my life (Ex. 3)	☐	☐	☐
▶ Give a presentation about "must-see" places in my city and explain my choices (Ex. 4)	☐	☐	☐

Now do the corresponding exercises. Was your assessment correct?

1 DISCUSSION
Likes and dislikes

A Look at these items. Can you think of a personal example for each one?

1. something you're into / not into doing by yourself
2. the kind of music you feel like listening to when you're in a bad mood
3. something you like doing when you're stressed out
4. a household chore you don't mind / can't stand doing
5. something you avoid doing, if possible

B Pair work Discuss your answers with a partner.

"I'm really into going to art galleries by myself. That way I can spend as much time as I want."

"Oh, I'm just the opposite. I don't really like going to galleries alone. It's nice to share the experience with someone."

2 DISCUSSION
The people's action committee

A Pair work You are members of an action group that has been asked to suggest improvements for your city. Make a list of changes you think should be made.

"We think the city shouldn't allow cars in the downtown area on weekends. It would be nice to be able to walk around without worrying about traffic."

B Group work Compare your recommendations in groups. Choose the four most interesting recommendations and share them with the class.

Useful expressions

Making recommendations

The city should provide . . .
The city ought to . . . because . . .
Wouldn't it be nice if . . . ?
It would make a lot of sense to . . .

3 LISTENING & SPEAKING
Who's sorry now?

A Listen to a radio show called *Who's Sorry Now?* What is the focus of the show? Choose the correct answer.

- ☐ a. people's roommates in college
- ☐ b. things that people should or should not have done in the past
- ☐ c. family vacations

B Listen again. Are these statements true or false? Choose the correct answer.

	True	False
1. Mark made the manager think that Luke didn't want the job.	☐	☐
2. Mark said he should feel terrible, but he doesn't.	☐	☐
3. Anna buried her brother's harmonica in the desert.	☐	☐
4. Anna said she should have bought her brother a drum set.	☐	☐
5. Luke didn't tell his roommate that he knew about the call.	☐	☐
6. Luke thinks he should have told his roommate he knew about the call.	☐	☐

C Pair work Have you ever made a mistake like the ones on the radio show? Would you consider calling a show like *Who's Sorry Now?* to talk about it?

"Have you ever made a mistake like the ones on the radio show?"

"Well, when I was in college, I used to make up excuses so that I could avoid going to French class. I should have gone. I really wish I could speak French now."

"Would you call up a show like Who's Sorry Now?*"*

"I don't know. Maybe it would be fun. What about you?"

4 DISCUSSION
Welcome to my city!

A What are three places in your city that people would enjoy visiting? Make a list.

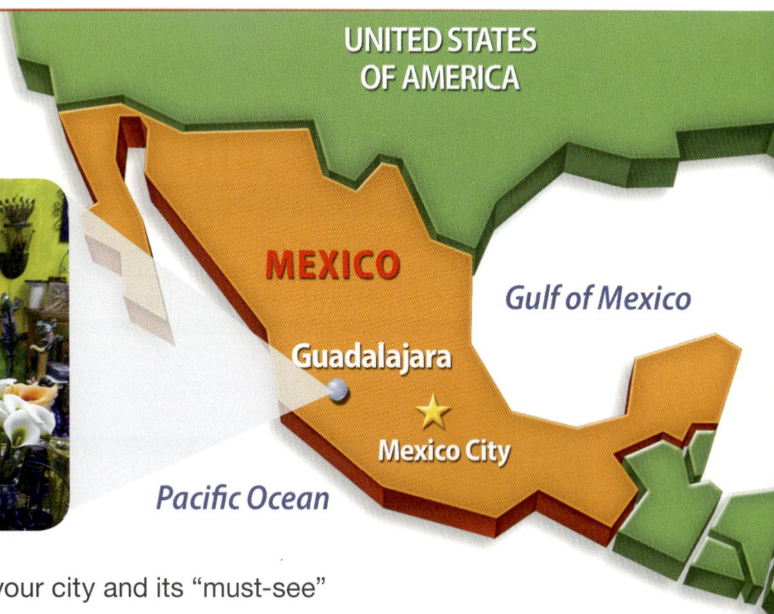

B Group work Tell your group facts about your city and its "must-see" places. Explain why they are worth seeing.

"Guadalajara, which is the second largest city in Mexico, has a lot of great markets. The Libertad Market is fantastic. It's a market every tourist should see because . . ."

4 EARLY BIRDS AND NIGHT OWLS

LESSON A ▶ *It's about time!*

1 STARTING POINT
What's your best time of day?

A Read these statements. How would you define the boldfaced words?

Teresa, South Africa

As soon as I get up in the morning, I race off to the gym. After I finish my workout, I head to the office. I always get there before any of my colleagues arrive. I suppose I'm a **morning person**.

Caio, Brazil

Ever since I was a kid, I've had trouble getting up early, so I guess I'm a **late riser**. Until I've had my coffee, I'm such a grouch. I'm not very approachable right after I wake up!

Mieko, Japan

I'm a **power napper**. While I take my lunch break at work, I often sneak a five-minute nap at my desk. After I have a little sleep, I feel great the rest of the day.

Richard, U.S.

I don't get much done until it gets to be late afternoon. Then I usually get a spurt of energy. I can concentrate best after everyone else has gone to bed. I'd say I'm a real **night owl**.

B Group work Which of the people in part A are you most similar to? Why?

2 DISCUSSION
The time is right.

A Pair work Read this information. Do you agree with the advice given? Why or why not?

When the Mind and Body Are at Their Best

- Get on social networking sites between **8:00 and 9:00 A.M.**, when people tend to post more positive messages.
- Whenever you need to study for a test, do it in the **late morning**, when most adults perform their best.
- Whenever you have to work with numbers, plan to do it around **noon**, when thinking power is at its peak.
- Energy levels drop between **1:00 and 4:00 P.M.**, and sleepiness is at its peak around **2:00 P.M.** This is a good time for a short nap.
- Exercise between **4:00 and 7:00 P.M.**, when physical strength is at its greatest and risk of injury is at its lowest.
- People can be most creative when they are less focused. Therefore, morning people are most creative in the evening, and night owls are most creative in the morning.

B Pair work Do you prefer to do these things in the morning, the afternoon, the evening, or at night? Why? Compare answers.

1. exercise 2. listen to music 3. study 4. speak English

3 GRAMMAR

Reduced time clauses

Notice how these clauses show time relationships. If the subject is the same in both clauses of the sentence, time clauses with *(right) before*, *(right) after*, and *while* can be reduced.

After I finish / **After** finishing my workout, I head to the office.
While I take / **While** taking my lunch break at work, I often sneak a five-minute nap.
I'm not very approachable **right after** I wake up / **right after** waking up!

However, other time clauses cannot usually be reduced.

Ever since I was a kid, I've had trouble getting up early.
As soon as I get up in the morning, I race off to the gym.
Until I've had my coffee, I'm such a grouch.
Whenever you have to work with numbers, plan to do it around noon.
I've been a night person **from the moment** I started college.

GRAMMAR PLUS *see page 112*

A Look at the Starting Point on page 28 again. Can you find more time clauses? Which one can be reduced?

B Pair work Complete the sentences with information about yourself. Then discuss your answers with a partner.

1. While working on a really difficult task, . . .
2. I don't feel awake in the morning until . . .
3. Whenever I have trouble sleeping, . . .
4. I can never concentrate after . . .
5. From the moment I wake up in the morning, . . .
6. As soon as I start to feel sleepy in the evening, . . .
7. Ever since I was young, . . .

"While working on a really difficult task, I have to stretch every 30 minutes."

4 VOCABULARY & SPEAKING

Energy and sleep

A Match the phrasal verb in the question with the correct definition.

1. Do you ever **burn out** from too much work? ____	a. become calm
2. How do you **calm down** after an argument? ____	b. get more energy
3. How do you **chill out** after a rough day? ____	c. go to bed
4. Do you ever **doze off** for a few minutes in public? ____	d. lose all your energy
5. How do you **perk up** when you feel sleepy? ____	e. fall asleep for a short time
6. Do you **race off** as soon as class is over? ____	f. take it easy
7. How often do you **sleep over** at a friend's? ____	g. stay for the night
8. What time do you **turn in** on the weekend? ____	h. go quickly

B Pair work Discuss the questions in part A. Ask follow-up questions.

"Whenever I feel like I'm going to burn out, I go for a bike ride to relax."
"That sounds like a good idea. Where do you like to ride?"

VOCABULARY PLUS *see page 133*

5 LISTENING & SPEAKING
Chilling out

A Stress can cause fatigue and a lack of energy. Select the things you do to cope with stress. Can you add other suggestions to the list?

☐ call a friend	☐ get a massage	☐ vent your feelings
☐ do yoga	☐ listen to music	☐ ______________
☐ exercise vigorously	☐ take a hot bath	☐ ______________

B Listen to Sean (*S*), Lisa (*L*), and Victor (*V*) talk about stress. What is the main cause of stress for each person? Write the correct letter.

____ too little time ____ too much traffic ____ too many responsibilities

C Listen again. What solution has each person found? Complete the chart.

	Solution
1. Sean	
2. Lisa	
3. Victor	

6 ROLE PLAY
I need some advice.

A Look at the problems below. Have you ever had problems like these? What other problems do people have with sleep and energy levels?

CALLER 1
I've been working day and night on an important project. It's going well, but I'm feeling so worn out. I'm worried about my health.

CALLER 2
I get so nervous before I have to give a presentation that I can't sleep the night before, and then I'm not at my best.

CALLER 3
I always put off studying until the night before a test. I stay up all night studying, but after that, I still don't do very well.

CALLER 4
Whenever my friends call or text me late at night, we chat for hours and hours. The next day, I can't keep my eyes open!

B Pair work Imagine you have one of the problems in part A. Take turns asking for and giving advice.

"I have a real problem. I've been working a lot on this project, and I'm so worn out. I'm worried about my health."
"So, how late do you usually work during the week?"
"I usually stay until 9:00 P.M. or so."
"Have you ever thought of telling someone that you need a little help?"

Useful expressions

Giving advice
Have you ever thought of (going) . . . ?
You might want to . . .
It might not be a bad idea to . . .
The way I see it, you ought to . . .

7 WRITING
Effective topic sentences

Effective topic sentences are neither too general nor too specific. A topic sentence is supported by the other sentences in the paragraph.

A Read the paragraph. Then choose the best topic sentence from the list.

______________________________ Morning people jump out of bed in the morning, cheerful and full of energy. They seem to get most of their work done before lunch. On the other hand, night people have trouble getting up in the morning. They often drag themselves through the day and reach their peak in the evening. Night people, who often stay up until 2:00 or 3:00 A.M., are just getting started when morning people are going to bed.

a. Early morning is a bad time of day for most people.
b. Morning people and night people live very different lives.
c. Working at night is hard for morning people.
d. Night people get enough sleep even though they go to bed late.

B Read the paragraph and complete the topic sentence. Then compare answers with a partner.

Playing sports ______________________________.
Usually, I play soccer or basketball. Kicking a soccer ball around clears my head. When I'm playing, I don't think about anything but the ball. Later, I feel relaxed, I'm focused, and I'm ready to concentrate on my homework.

C Choose one of these topics or your own idea. Then write a paragraph with a topic sentence.

- the best way to stay healthy
- an effective study plan
- earning extra money

D **Pair work** Take turns reading your paragraphs out loud, but don't read the topic sentence. Can you guess what your partner's topic sentence is?

LESSON B ▶ *Tossing and turning*

1 STARTING POINT
A good night's sleep

A Read the statements about sleep habits. Choose the statements that are true for you.

- [ ] I sometimes lie awake at night, even if I'm really tired.
- [ ] I'm lucky I can get by on six hours of sleep, considering that most people need eight.
- [ ] I'm a light sleeper, so any little noise wakes me up unless I'm really tired.
- [ ] I can manage on five hours of sleep, as long as I take a nap during the day.
- [ ] Unless I get a good night's sleep, I can easily fall asleep at school, at work, or even on the bus.
- [ ] I always set two alarm clocks just in case one of them doesn't go off.
- [ ] I only wake up early if I have somewhere to be in the morning.
- [ ] I never have any trouble sleeping.
- [ ] I'm exhausted every morning, even if I slept great all night.

B Pair work Compare your answers. Which statements are true for you?

"I definitely lie awake at night, even if I'm really tired. I can't help it. I replay everything that happened during the day."

"You're not the only one. I do the same thing, especially when I'm feeling stressed."

2 VOCABULARY
Expressions related to sleep

A Put these expressions about sleep in the correct columns. Then compare answers.

be fast asleep	be wide awake	feel drowsy	nod off	take a power nap
be sound asleep	drift off	have a sleepless night	sleep like a log	toss and turn

Having trouble sleeping	Falling asleep	Sleeping a short time	Sleeping deeply
			be fast asleep

B Pair work Use the expressions in part A to discuss your sleep habits and suggestions about sleeping better.

"Do you ever take a power nap during the day?"

"Not really. Whenever I try to take a nap, I end up sleeping until the next morning. But let me ask you something. What do you do when you feel drowsy after lunch?"

VOCABULARY PLUS *see page 133*

3 GRAMMAR

Clauses stating reasons and conditions

Even if **introduces a condition that does not influence the main clause.**
I sometimes lie awake at night, **even if** I'm really tired.

Considering that **introduces causes and reasons that explain the main clause.**
I'm lucky I can get by on six hours of sleep, **considering that** most people need eight.

As long as **introduces a condition on which the main clause depends.**
I can manage on five hours of sleep, **as long as** I take a nap during the day.

Unless **introduces something that must happen in order to avoid a consequence.**
Unless I get a good night's sleep, I can easily fall asleep at school, at work, or even on the bus.

(Just) in case **introduces an undesirable circumstance that needs to be taken into account.**
I always set two alarm clocks **(just) in case** one of them doesn't go off.

Only if **or** ***only . . . if*** **introduces a condition that must be met for the main clause to be true.**
I **only** wake up early **if** I have somewhere to be in the morning.
I wake up early **only if** I have somewhere to be in the morning.

GRAMMAR PLUS *see page 113*

A Look at the Starting Point on page 32 again. Can you find more clauses stating reasons and conditions?

B Match the clauses to make sentences. Then compare answers with a partner.

1. Drivers can fall asleep on the highway ____
2. Power naps at work are a good idea, ____
3. Some people set two morning alarms ____
4. I was surprisingly alert at work, ____
5. Night owls hate to wake up early, ____
6. I drink hot milk before bed only ____

a. if I've been having trouble sleeping.
b. even if it's a beautiful morning.
c. unless they rest before long trips.
d. as long as you have your boss's OK.
e. considering that I didn't sleep at all last night.
f. in case they sleep through one.

C Complete the sentences with information about yourself. Then compare answers with a partner.

1. Unless I have enough sleep at night, . . .
   I can't think very clearly in the morning.
2. I usually wake up on time, as long as . . .
3. I fall asleep pretty quickly at night, considering that . . .
4. I always have a boring book on my night table just in case . . .
5. Even if I'm extremely stressed out, I never . . .
6. I only leave a light on if . . .

4 LISTENING & SPEAKING
I had the wildest dream.

A Listen to Kate and Sérgio talk about their recurring dreams. Whose dream do you think is scarier?

B Listen again. What is each person's dream? What do they think the dreams mean? Complete the chart.

	Dream	Meaning
Kate		
Sérgio		

C Pair work What do you think their dreams mean? Do you ever have similar dreams?

5 DISCUSSION
The meaning of dreams

A Read the information. Match the dreams with their possible meanings.

DREAMS

1. **Falling** You are falling through space, but you don't hit the ground or hurt yourself. ___
2. **Flying** You are flying and enjoying the sensation. ___
3. **Being chased** You feel as if someone is chasing you and you're in danger. ___
4. **Being embraced** Someone you like approaches you and hugs you. ___
5. **Losing teeth** Your teeth all fall out suddenly. ___
6. **Winning** You are successful in doing something. ___
7. **Being ashamed** You do something embarrassing and feel ashamed. ___

MEANINGS

a. You like someone and feel you can trust that person.
b. You feel very optimistic and proud about how your life is going.
c. You feel pleased with yourself and superior to other people.
d. You feel disappointed in yourself because of something you did.
e. You are worried about something, and this is a warning to be careful.
f. You feel out of control because someone is threatening you.
g. You feel insecure, and you are worried about losing something.

B Pair work Read these accounts of unusual dreams. What do you think they mean?

"Suddenly I found myself on stage in a school play and realized that I didn't know my lines. . . ."

"I was in a hot-air balloon above a big park. When I looked down, I was amazed to see hundreds of people on the ground pointing up at me. . . ."

"I was in a strange country and didn't know how I'd gotten there. I asked a man for help, and he held up a sign in a language I'd never seen before. . . ."

Useful expressions

Interpreting meaning

I think that means . . .
It sounds like . . .
The (balloon) probably stands for . . .
It might symbolize . . .

C Group work Finish each of the dreams. Take turns adding sentences.

6 READING

To sleep or not to sleep?

A Group work How many hours do you think people should sleep? Why? Discuss with your group. Then read the article.

In the days before electricity, people didn't worry much about sleep. They usually went to bed a couple of hours after sunset and woke at sunrise. Even if they stayed up, there wasn't much to do in those days after the sun went down. But then came the electric lightbulb. And now we have the Internet, smartphones, stores that are open 24/7, and longer hours at work. How much can we sleep? How much should we sleep?

Like it or not, many of us are sleeping less on average. In 1910, most Americans slept nine hours a night. That dropped to seven hours by 2001. In 2009, a study by the National Sleep Foundation found that the average American got only 6.7 hours of sleep. The news is even worse for people who work the night shift. They sleep an average of just five hours.

Are we sleeping enough? Not if you believe in the old formula of eight hours of rest, eight hours of work, and eight hours of play. On the other hand, Neil Stanley, a British scientist who studies sleep, believes people's sleep needs vary. Some people need as many as 11 hours, but others need as few as three. How much do you really need? "To find out," he says, "simply sleep until you wake naturally, without the aid of an alarm clock. Feel rested? That's your sleep need."

Meanwhile, other scientists and pharmaceutical researchers are searching for new ways to keep us awake longer and prevent us from nodding off. A group of scientists is studying a gene found in some fruit flies that lets them get by on one-third the usual amount of sleep. Other researchers are developing chemicals that are more powerful than caffeine, the chemical found in coffee and tea. One experimental drug, CX717, kept laboratory monkeys working happily and accurately for 36 hours. Future breakthroughs may allow people to stay wide awake for several days straight.

The implications of this research are huge. On the one hand, this could lead to a world where we work longer and longer hours with less and less sleep. On the other hand, if we needed less sleep, we would have more free time for travel, sports, personal goals, and family.

To sleep or not to sleep – that may soon be the question.

B Read the article again. Then answer the questions.

1. What scientific research is mentioned in the article? What surprised you the most? What surprised you the least?
2. How much sleep does Neil Stanley think a person needs? Why?
3. What effects did the experimental drug mentioned in the article have on laboratory animals?

C Group work Discuss these questions. Then share your answers with the class.

1. Do you think you get enough sleep? What things keep you from getting more?
2. What do you think would happen if scientists found ways to let people stay awake longer? Would people be happier? Explain your answers.

5 COMMUNICATION

LESSON A ► *Making conversation*

1 STARTING POINT

Types of people you might meet

A Read about six different types of people you sometimes meet on social occasions. Match the descriptions with the pictures.

1. It's a good idea to try out different topics to get a conversation going, and the **conversation starter** does just that. ____
2. Talking about your accomplishments too much is often considered rude, but that doesn't stop the **braggart**. ____
3. Saying nice things about others is customary for the **complimenter**. ____
4. It's rude to ignore your conversation partner, but the **wandering mind** does it anyway. ____
5. Talking about topics that interest you is fun. Unfortunately, the **bore** is interesting to no one else. ____
6. It's usually considered impolite to interrupt people, but the **interrupter** is always jumping into the conversation out of turn. ____

B Pair work Do you know any people like the six types above? What is it like to have a conversation with them?

"My best friend is kind of an interrupter. She's really nice, but I guess she just gets excited about the conversation and wants to jump in. It can be very annoying."

2 GRAMMAR

Infinitive and gerund phrases

***It* + *be* + adjective/noun + infinitive phrase is often used to comment on behavior. These sentences can also be restated with gerund phrases.**

It's rude to ignore your conversation partner.	**Ignoring** your conversation partner **is rude**.
It's a good idea to try out different topics.	**Trying out** different topics **is a good idea**.

The word *considered* may also follow *be* in this kind of sentence.

It's considered impolite to interrupt people.	**Interrupting** people **is considered impolite**.

These sentences can also include the phrase *for* + person/pronoun.

It's customary for the complimenter to say nice things about others.	Saying nice things about others **is customary for the complimenter**.

GRAMMAR PLUS *see page 114*

A Look at the Starting Point on page 36 again. Can you find more sentences that begin with gerunds? Try to change them into sentences beginning with *it's*.

B Rewrite the sentences using infinitive or gerund phrases. Then compare answers with a partner.

1. It's inappropriate to talk about politics at work or school.
   Talking about politics at work or school is inappropriate.
2. Using certain gestures is impolite in some foreign countries.
3. Asking someone's age is often considered rude.
4. It's not unusual in the U.S. to address a professor by his or her first name.
5. Hugging friends when you greet them is customary in many cultures.
6. Asking strangers if they're married is inappropriate in some countries.

3 VOCABULARY & SPEAKING

What's appropriate?

A Are these words and phrases positive (+), negative (–), or neutral (~)? Write the correct symbol next to each word.

____ 1. a compliment	____ 4. bad form	____ 7. offensive	____ 10. strange
____ 2. an insult	____ 5. inappropriate	____ 8. polite	____ 11. typical
____ 3. appropriate	____ 6. normal	____ 9. rude	____ 12. unusual

B Group work How do you feel about these things? Discuss these situations using the words and phrases in part A.

1. You kiss people on the cheek when you meet them.
2. You and your classmates interrupt the teacher.
3. You stand very close to people when you talk to them.
4. You and your parents talk honestly and openly.
5. Your best friend calls you after 11:00 P.M.
6. You start a conversation with a stranger on a bus or subway.

"It's unusual for me to kiss people I meet on the cheek."

VOCABULARY PLUS *see page 134*

4 ROLE PLAY
Making small talk

A Small talk is light conversation, often between people who don't know each other. Select the topics that are appropriate for small talk in your culture.

What's Safe for Small Talk?

- [ ] Children and family
- [ ] Current affairs
- [ ] Entertainment
- [ ] Health problems
- [ ] Hobbies
- [ ] Marital status
- [ ] Salaries
- [ ] Sports
- [ ] The weather

B **Group work** Imagine you are at a party. Start a conversation with one person, keep it going for one minute, and bring it to a close. Then find a new partner and repeat.

"Hi. How's it going?"
"Pretty good. Hey, did you see that soccer game last night?"
"I did! It's amazing to see our team play so well."
"I know! Hey, I should get going, but I'll call you later."

Useful expressions

Conversation openers	Conversation closers
How's it going?	See you later.
Can you believe this weather? It's (awful)!	Sorry, I've got to run. Talk to you soon.
That's a great (jacket).	It was great to meet you.
Do you know many people here?	I should get going. I'll call you later.

5 LISTENING
Party talk

A Listen to three conversations at different parties. Who is speaking in each one?

1. a. a mother and her son
   b. a teacher and her student
   c. a woman and her son's friend
2. a. two young students
   b. two older friends
   c. a father and his son
3. a. two cooks
   b. two wives
   c. two classmates

B Listen again. What closing phrase is used to end each conversation?

1. ______________________ 2. ______________________ 3. ______________________

6 WRITING
Organizing ideas with an outline

Making an outline is a good way to organize your ideas before you write. An outline is usually written in reduced sentences or in notes and provides a general plan to follow when you write.

A Read the paragraph about a cultural rule in Japan. Then complete the outline below with information from the paragraph. What additional information is included in the paragraph but not in the outline?

Speaking on a cell phone in some public places in Japan is considered impolite. When receiving or making a cell phone call, most Japanese step away from the people around them. If that's impossible, it's customary to speak softly and use your hand to cover your mouth. Announcements on Japanese trains constantly remind passengers to switch their phones to silent mode. This is because people dislike being bothered by noise. Not everyone follows the rules, but most people do. The other day, people were glaring at me for taking a call in a café, and one person even scolded me. I was pretty shocked, but then I thought about it. Listening to others talking on the phone is irritating. There is a good reason why Japanese people use polite behavior when speaking on cell phones.

A. Topic sentence

Speaking on a cell phone in some public places in Japan is impolite.

B. Supporting sentences

- Recommended behavior:
  ______________ *or speak softly and cover mouth*
- General example:
  Train announcements remind passengers – put phone on silent
- Personal example:
  People glaring for taking a call in ______________

C. Concluding sentence

There is a good reason why Japanese people ______________.

B Pair work Write an outline about a cultural rule from your country. Then exchange outlines and answer the questions.

1. Is the outline in a logical order?
2. Does the outline provide enough information? Is there anything else you would include?

C Pair work Use your outline to write a paragraph about the cultural rule. Then exchange paragraphs and answer the questions.

1. Does the paragraph follow the outline?
2. Is the cultural rule clear? What suggestions do you have to make it clearer?

LESSON B ▶ *It's personal.*

1 STARTING POINT
Eavesdroppers

A Read each person's statement. What do you think they should do about each situation?

I Wish I Hadn't Heard That!

Luis, 23, Mexico City

"On the bus to work, I heard my boss's voice behind me. I think he was talking to the office manager on his cell phone. He was telling her that it would be a bad day at work. He explained that they were going to lay off my entire department!"

Rebecca, 25, Vancouver

"I overheard my roommate and her friend gossiping about me when I got home. I asked them what they were saying, but they claimed they hadn't been talking about me. I knew that wasn't true. It really hurt my feelings."

Pam, 18, Portland

"Last week, I overheard my little brother on his cell phone. He was warning his friend not to say anything. So of course I listened. He said he was getting a terrible grade in math this year! And he said it was a big secret, too. In fact, my parents still don't know the truth."

B Group work Have you ever heard someone talking about you? What did you do?

2 DISCUSSION
Who can you confide in?

A Read the information in the chart. Would you rank each person in the same way?

Who do you tell first?

We asked a group of young adults to rate each person in the chart according to when they would tell that person different types of personal news (1 = tell first, 4 = tell last). This is what they said.

Who would you tell . . .	Family member	Spouse	Close friend	Colleague
good news?	2	1	3	4
bad/tragic news?	1	2	3	4
gossip?	4	3	2	1
personal information?	3	2	1	4

Source: Interviews with people between the ages of 22 and 35

B Pair work Why would you tell something to one person and not to another? Discuss your reasons.

"I would usually talk about a personal problem with my close friends rather than my colleagues because my friends already know most of my secrets."

3 GRAMMAR

Reported speech

Statements	Reported statements
"It'**s** a big secret."	He said (that) it **was** a big secret.
"I'**m getting** a terrible grade."	He said (that) he **was getting** a terrible grade.
"They **got** engaged."	He said (that) they **had gotten** engaged.
"We **weren't talking** about you."	They claimed (that) they **hadn't been talking** about me.
"She'**s been** absent since Tuesday."	He said (that) she **had been** absent since Tuesday.
"We **had never been** there before."	She said (that) they **had never been** there before.
"I'**ll meet** you at the café."	He said (that) he **would meet** me at the café.
Questions	**Reported questions**
"**Did** you **know** about the layoffs?"	I asked him if he **had known** about the layoffs.
"What **are** you **saying**?"	I asked them what they **were saying**.
Commands	**Reported commands**
"**Don't say** anything!"	He warned his friend **not to say** anything.
General truths	**Reported general truths**
"The sun **rises** in the east."	She said (that) the sun **rises** in the east. (*No change in tense.*)

GRAMMAR PLUS *see page 115*

A Look at the Starting Point on page 40 again. Can you find more examples of reported speech?

B Rewrite the sentences using reported speech. Then compare answers with a partner.

1. "I'm not surprised at all." She told me ______________________.
2. "Have you heard the news?" He asked me ______________________.
3. "There's a bank down the street." She said ______________________.
4. "Why aren't you talking?" She asked me ______________________.
5. "Give him a call!" He told me ______________________.
6. "We're getting married!" She told me ______________________.
7. "Was the movie scary?" The children asked me ______________________.
8. "We didn't take the 8:00 train." They told me ______________________.

C Pair work Imagine that you have overheard this conversation. Take turns reporting each line of the conversation.

Ryan: I heard some interesting news. Do you know Amanda Jenkins?
Lara: I know what she looks like, but I've never met her.
Ryan: Well, she's going to study for a year in Australia.
Lara: How can she afford that?
Ryan: She got a scholarship that will take care of all her expenses.
Lara: I think that's great. When is she leaving?
Ryan: I don't know . . .

"Ryan told Lara that he'd heard some interesting news. He . . ."

4 VOCABULARY & SPEAKING

Tell me what he said.

A Put these expressions for reported speech in the correct columns.

He claimed that . . .	He promised to . . .	He told me that . . .	He advised me to . . .
He asked me to . . .	He wanted to know . . .	He told me to . . .	He encouraged me to . . .
He warned me not to . . .	He explained that . . .	He asked me . . .	He wondered . . .

Statements	Commands or advice	Questions
He claimed that . . .		

B Pair work Tell a partner about a conversation you recently had. What was said? Use one of these topics or your own idea.

- an argument you had with a friend
- a time you asked someone for a big favor
- some exciting news a friend told you
- an apology you made or received

"My roommate claimed I had borrowed her sweater without asking, but I explained that . . ."

VOCABULARY PLUS *see page 134*

5 LISTENING

Tell me all about it!

A Listen to Nicole's and Tony's news. Choose the correct pictures.

1. Nicole

a. ☐

b. ☐

2. Tony

a. ☐

b. ☐

B Listen again. Choose the best answers.

1. Nicole's sister met her boyfriend . . .
   - ☐ a. in the fall.
   - ☐ b. yesterday.
   - ☐ c. over four years ago.
2. Nicole's sister is probably . . .
   - ☐ a. not afraid to be different.
   - ☐ b. very traditional.
   - ☐ c. shy.
3. How are things at the design studio?
   - ☐ a. There isn't enough work.
   - ☐ b. Things are picking up.
   - ☐ c. Everything's about the same.
4. Tony has been working at the studio . . .
   - ☐ a. longer than most other workers.
   - ☐ b. less time than most other workers.
   - ☐ c. as long as most other workers.

6 READING

Mobile mania

A Read the article. These headings are missing from the text. Put them in the correct place.

The Generic Ring	The Distracted Driver	The Useless Call Maker
The I-Talk-Anywhere	The Shouter	The Corporate Big Shot

CELL PHONE PERSONALITY TYPES

In her travels, "Telephone Doctor" Nancy Friedman has noticed a variety of "cell phone personalities." Which of these types have you seen around?

1. *The Shouter*

Talking three times louder than necessary is characteristic of this offensive cell phone user. He seems to think everyone has a hearing impairment. Doesn't he know the phone already amplifies his voice?

2. ______

This pompous fellow makes all his business calls in public places while standing in the middle of a crowded room. He conducts big business deals right there in front of us, but we're not impressed.

3. ______

This exasperating person makes trivial phone calls, one after another, after another. On airplanes, you'll overhear her saying ridiculous things like, "Hi, we haven't left yet," or "Hi, we just landed. OK, see you in a minute."

4. ______

Making and taking calls anytime, anywhere is the trademark of this infuriating person. She'll chat in restaurants, at movie theaters, and even at funerals. When her cell phone rings, she looks at you and says insincerely, "Oh, sorry about that."

5. ______

Drive or use the phone – don't do both at the same time. This can be dangerous. It's really scary to see a delivery truck in the rearview mirror with a distracted driver on a phone behind the wheel.

6. ______

These are the people who haven't bothered to personalize their ring tone. One phone rings and 10 people check to see if it's theirs. Hang on, I think that's my phone!

Source: "What Type of Cell Phone User Are You?" by Nancy Friedman, www.telephonedoctor.com

B Group work Does the article describe any cell phone users you know or have seen? What bad cell phone manners have you seen recently?

6 WHAT'S THE REAL STORY?

LESSON A ▶ *That's some story!*

1 STARTING POINT
Weird news

A Read the news articles. Match each headline with the correct article.

a **CELL PHONE** *OPENS* **CAR DOOR**

b **SEA LION** Paints for Her Supper

c **SURFING DOG** Upstages Rivals

1 ☐ The police have been called to a surfing contest in Brazil because a dog has been stealing all the attention. The dog became the main attraction at Praia da Tiririca in Bahia during the Surf World Championship. The dog and his owner surfed together on the same surfboard between the competitions. Police said, "They've called us to remove the pair because they've been getting more attention than the actual contest." The dog's owner said, "I've always surfed with my dog. He's always loved it. Sometimes I think he's a better surfer than I am!"

2 ☐ Maggie, a California sea lion at the Pittsburgh Zoo, has been amazing visitors by painting for her supper. She has created dozens of paintings. Her trainer said, "I started teaching her to paint last year, and she caught on quickly." Maggie spent three months learning to hold the paintbrush in her mouth and to touch it to the canvas. Adding the paint was the next step. Maggie earned a fish for every successful brushstroke. The trainer has saved all the paintings. She'll probably sell them to raise money to help animals.

3 ☐

A shopper in Michigan saved time and money after her husband helped her unlock her car from 10 miles away. After a day at the mall, the woman went out to her car, but couldn't find her keys. When she saw them still in the ignition, she called home and said, "I've locked my keys in the car. I've never done that before. I don't know what to do." Following her husband's instructions, she held her cell phone about a foot from the car door, while her husband held the spare car remote near his phone and pressed the unlock button. The door unlocked. She said, "I've totally stopped worrying about my keys now."

B Pair work One of the news stories isn't true. Which one do you think it is? (For the answer, see page 142.)

"I think story number one has got to be false. I just don't believe that a dog could surf. Story number two is also pretty amazing, but I have a feeling it's true."

2 GRAMMAR

Present perfect vs. simple past

Use the present perfect to report a recent event without giving a specific time reference.
I**'ve locked** my keys in the car.

Use the simple past to report an event with a specific time reference.
After a day at the mall, the woman **went out** to her car.
I **started** teaching her to paint **last year**.

GRAMMAR PLUS *see page 116*

A Look at the first story on page 44 again. Can you find more examples of the present perfect and the simple past? Why is each tense used?

B Complete the news story with the present perfect or simple past form of the verbs in parentheses. Then compare answers with a partner.

A group of thieves (1) *has stolen* (steal) the Dragon's Eye ruby from the Grand Gallery. Last night at about 1:00 A.M., the alarm (2) __________ (go off). Police (3) __________ (rush) to the building immediately, but they (4) __________ (be) too late. Right after learning of the robbery, the mayor (5) __________ (set up) a telephone hotline for information about the theft. Three people (6) __________ (call) so far, but the police are still looking for further information. They believe it is probable that the thieves (7) __________ (leave) the city. The curator of the Grand Gallery (8) __________ (offer) a $50,000 reward for information leading to the capture of the thieves.

3 GRAMMAR

Present perfect vs. present perfect continuous

Use the present perfect continuous to describe temporary situations and actions that are not yet completed. The present perfect describes permanent situations and recently completed actions.
A dog **has been stealing** all the attention. *(temporary situation)*
I**'ve** always **surfed** with my dog. *(permanent situation)*
Maggie **has been amazing** visitors by painting for her supper. *(not yet completed action)*
I**'ve locked** my keys in the car. *(recently completed action)*

Use the present perfect with the passive or with stative verbs such as *be*, *love*, and *have*.
He**'s** always **loved** it.

GRAMMAR PLUS *see page 116*

A Look at the first story on page 44 again. Can you find another example of the present perfect continuous? Why is this form used?

B Complete the sentences with the present perfect or present perfect continuous form of the verbs in parentheses. Then compare answers with a partner.

1. Many residents *have been* (be) homeless ever since last month's storm and __________ (stay) with relatives while their homes are being repaired.
2. Although crews __________ (repair) the subway signals all week, they still __________ (not solve) the problem of long delays.
3. Police __________ (guard) the stores that the thieves __________ (not rob) yet.
4. Some organizations __________ (provide) free meals to residents, and will continue to do so all week.

4 VOCABULARY & SPEAKING
It's in the news.

A How would you define each of these news events?

epidemic	hijacking	natural disaster	rebellion	robbery
famine	kidnapping	political crisis	recession	scandal

"A natural disaster is something like a volcanic eruption, a flood, or an earthquake."

B Pair work Tell your partner about some news stories you've recently heard. Use the words in part A.

"I saw something about a big scandal on the news this morning."
"Really? What was it?"
"Well, it said that a politician had been arrested for taking bribes."

VOCABULARY PLUS *see page 135*

5 LISTENING
Broadcast news

A Listen to an early morning news broadcast. What is each story about? Write the correct number.

____ a natural disaster ____ a scandal ____ an unusual family event ____ an epidemic

B Listen again. Are the statements true or false? Choose the correct answer. Then correct the false statements to make them true.

	True	False
1. More people are suffering from TB than ever before.	☐	☐
2. Standard TB drugs are ineffective in about one-fourth of cases.	☐	☐
3. The painting *Sunflowers* was purchased by a large company.	☐	☐
4. The high price paid for the painting caused a scandal.	☐	☐
5. The hurricane has trapped some people in their homes.	☐	☐
6. Tourism in the area hit by the hurricane will not be affected.	☐	☐
7. The mother left the house to give her children freedom.	☐	☐
8. The children used food to get their mom down from the tree.	☐	☐

6 SPEAKING
Speaking of the news

A Pair work Discuss the questions. Ask follow-up questions and add extra information.

1. How closely do you follow the news? What kinds of stories interest you?
2. What do you think was the most important news story in the last few years?
3. Do you think stories about sports or celebrities count as "real news"?

B Group work Compare your answers with another pair. How are your opinions about the news different?

7 WRITING
Narratives

A narrative is usually organized in chronological order and uses a variety of verb tenses.

A Number the events in this news story in the correct order. Then write a title for the article.

Title: ______________________________

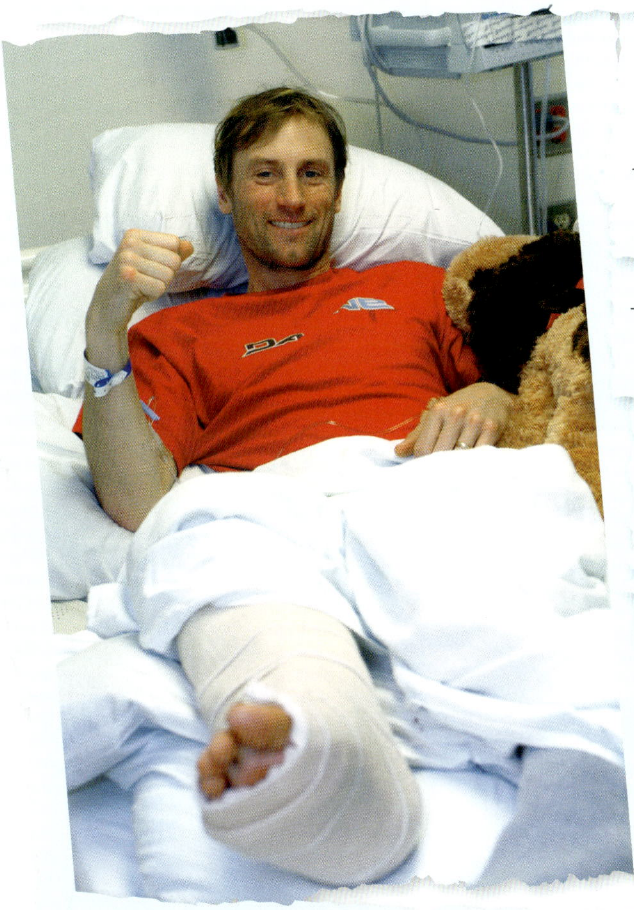

_____ As he was punching the shark, it began to release its grip on his leg.

_____ When the stunned shark finally let go, Anderson swam to shore, dragging his badly wounded leg behind him.

_____ He was pulling himself up on the rocks when another surfer came to his aid and called an ambulance.

_____ Anderson's leg was bleeding badly when emergency workers arrived, so they took him to a local hospital, where he was kept overnight for observation.

_____ In an interview shortly after Brian came home, his wife, also a surfer, said she knew her husband would surf again. However, she didn't know if she wanted her son to ever go back in the water!

_____ Doctors released Anderson the next day, and he spent the afternoon at home with his wife and son.

_2_ Realizing it was a shark, he punched it repeatedly in the nose so it would loosen its grip.

_1_ Brian Anderson was surfing at a popular spot south of Seaside, Oregon, on December 24, when he felt something was grabbing his leg.

_____ Anderson said he did this automatically because he'd heard on a TV show that sharks' noses are sensitive.

B Write a brief news story about a recent event. Use the simple past, present perfect, and present perfect continuous to show the order of events.

C **Group work** Take turns reading your stories. Ask follow-up questions. Who has the most interesting story? Why?

LESSON B ▶ *Storytelling*

1 STARTING POINT
What happened?

A Pair work Read the stories. What do you think happened? Choose two stories and complete them by filling in the gaps indicated by ~~~▶.

1

I went to the wrong class. It was the first day, so ~~~▶. Afterwards, a classmate told me it was French IV and not my class, French I.

2

I'd picked up my mother's ring at the jeweler, but I couldn't find it when I got home. Up until then, I had never lost anything important, so I ~~~▶. So, the ring wasn't lost after all! What a relief!

3

On my way home, I tried to take a shortcut through a neighbor's yard. As soon as I went through the gate, a huge dog suddenly ran up to me and ~~~▶. Afterwards, we all laughed about it.

4

I had left for work a little earlier than usual. I got to the subway station, and ~~~▶. When I got to work, my boss asked to speak to me. I knew he would never believe why I was late.

5

I volunteered to take care of my nephew. Before that, I'd never taken care of a toddler. As soon as his parents left, ~~~▶. When they finally got home, the apartment, my nephew, and I were a mess!

6

Until some good friends invited me to a sushi restaurant, I had never had sushi in my life. When I put the first piece in my mouth, ~~~▶. They were really nice about it, though.

B Group work Take turns sharing your stories. Have you had similar experiences?

2 LISTENING
How did it all end?

A Listen to two stories from the Starting Point. Which stories are they?

B Listen again. Choose the correct ending of each story.

1. ☐ a. He found the ring in his pocket.
   ☐ b. The jeweler had the ring.
   ☐ c. His mother found the ring.

2. ☐ a. The conductor helped her.
   ☐ b. A passenger helped her.
   ☐ c. The door finally opened.

3 GRAMMAR

Adverbs with the simple past and past perfect

Use these adverbs with the simple past to describe something that happened at a later time.
Afterwards, / Later, / The next day, we all **laughed** about it.

Use these adverbs with the simple past to describe two things that happened at the same time.
When / As soon as / The moment I **got** to work, my boss **asked** to speak to me.

Use these adverbs with the past perfect to describe something that was true or that happened before another event in the past.
Up until then, / Before that, / Until that time, I **had** never **lost** anything important.

GRAMMAR PLUS *see page 117*

A Look at the Starting Point on page 48 again. Can you find the adverbs from the grammar box? Which verb tenses are used after them?

B Write two sentences for these situations using the adverbs from the grammar box. Then compare answers with a partner.

1. My apartment was robbed last week.
   Up until then, I had never had anything stolen. The moment it happened, I called the police.
2. I moved into my own apartment this summer.
3. I failed my driving test last week.
4. I really enjoyed my trip to Singapore last month.
5. I was nervous about going to the dentist.
6. I knew I shouldn't have lent my friend my new laptop.

C Match the sentences with the illustrations. Then compare answers with a partner.

a

b

_b_ 1. This morning, I was on my way to work.
___ 2. Last night, I was telling a joke at a dinner party.
___ 3. I was backing my car out of the garage. I crashed into my neighbor's car.
___ 4. I got to the punch line. I knocked over a glass of water with my hand.
___ 5. She had never parked in front of my driveway.
___ 6. I noticed everyone laughing. I wasn't sure if they were laughing at the joke or at me.

D Pair work Take turns telling the stories for each picture. Use adverbs to show the order of events.

"This morning, I was on my way to work. I was backing my car out of the garage when I crashed into my neighbor's car. I couldn't believe it! Until then, she had . . ."

4 LISTENING
Embarrassing moments

A Listen to an interview with actor Dan Carville. What jobs does he talk about?

1. ____________ 2. ____________ 3. ____________

B Listen again. Answer the questions.

1. Why did Dan lose his job at the department store?
2. Why didn't Dan last long as a painter?
3. Why was Dan fired from his job as a taxi driver?
4. How seriously do you think Dan took these jobs?

5 VOCABULARY & SPEAKING
Creating a story

A These phrases are used to tell a story. Put them in the correct columns.

I'll never forget the time . . .
The thing you have to know is . . .
It all started when . . .
What happened was . . .
I forgot to mention that . . .
Meanwhile . . .
And in the end . . .
That reminds me of when . . .
The next thing we knew . . .
So later on . . .
To make a long story short . . .
I've got to tell you about . . .
The other thing is . . .
So finally . . .

Beginning a story	Continuing a story	Going back in a story	Ending a story
I'll never forget the time . . .			

B **Pair work** Tell a story about yourself. Use these story ideas and the phrases in part A. Ask follow-up questions.

STORY IDEAS

- You tried something for the first time.
- You did something really exciting.
- You forgot something important.
- You had a surprising experience.
- You met an unusual person.

"I'll never forget the first time I cooked a big dinner by myself. I had always helped my mother cook, so I thought it would be easy."

"Why were you cooking a big dinner?"

"Well, I had invited all my friends over, and . . ."

C **Group work** Share your story with another pair of students. Then choose one of the stories and tell it to the class.

VOCABULARY PLUS *see page 135*

6 READING
Personal anecdotes

A Pair work Look at the titles of the anecdotes. What do you think each one is about? Read the anecdotes to check your answers.

IT HAPPENED TO ME!
(or my friend . . . or a friend of a friend . . .)

Babysitter's Blues

I'll never forget the time last winter when I was babysitting these two kids for the first time. It was about 7:30 at night. Their mom had asked me to make them a pizza for dinner. It had been in the oven for about 15 minutes when suddenly I heard a noise outside, and the dog started barking. As soon as I opened the door and stepped outside, the kids slammed and locked it behind me. It was winter, and I stood outside freezing while they rolled around on the floor laughing hysterically. Meanwhile, the kitchen started getting smoky, and the smoke detector started buzzing. They didn't know what to do, so they let me back in. The pizza was burnt to a crisp. I didn't say anything. But, as we sat around the kitchen table having a bowl of cold cereal instead of their favorite, pizza, I could tell they regretted what they'd done. Anyway, to make a long story short, I babysit them all the time now, and guess what. I haven't had any problems since that first night.

– Amy Fernandez, Boston

A Bad Holiday

Have I learned any lessons the hard way? I sure have! What happened was I wanted a Monday off from work. Tuesday was a national holiday, and I thought a four-day weekend would be just perfect. I asked my boss, and he said no. At that company, all employees got their birthday off, so I asked if we could pretend that the Monday was my birthday. He said no. I woke up on the Monday morning feeling a little defiant, so I called in sick. I told them I got a terrible sunburn on the weekend. Later on, I realized that I had no color at all because I hadn't been out in the sun. So my friends and I went to the beach and stayed there all day. When I woke up the next morning, I had the worst sunburn of my life. I even had to go to the hospital! In the end, I learned a valuable lesson – I can't get away with anything!

– Rita Wagner, San Diego

B Group work Discuss these questions. Then share your answers with the class.

1. Why do you think Amy hasn't had any more problems?
2. What would you have done if you were Rita?
3. Which anecdote did you find more amusing? Why?

C Group work Choose one of the topics below, or one of your own, and tell your group an anecdote. Who had the most interesting anecdote? Whose was the funniest?

- celebrity encounters
- childhood memories
- food experiences
- mistaken identity
- school days
- speaking English
- strange coincidences
- travel stories

COMMUNICATION REVIEW
UNITS 4–6

SELF-ASSESSMENT

How well can you do these things? Choose the best answer.

I can . . .	Very well	OK	A little
▸ Describe how I deal with everyday problems (Ex. 1)	☐	☐	☐
▸ Describe a conversation I've heard or participated in (Ex. 2)	☐	☐	☐
▸ Understand the main points of an academic presentation about stress (Ex. 3)	☐	☐	☐
▸ Evaluate suggestions in a discussion about ways to deal with stress (Ex. 3)	☐	☐	☐
▸ Tell an interesting anecdote from my life (Ex. 4)	☐	☐	☐

Now do the corresponding exercises. Was your assessment correct?

1 SPEAKING
Calm down, chill out.

A What do you do in these situations?

1. Tomorrow is a big day – you have a job interview or an exam. You are worried that you won't sleep well.
2. You've been lying in bed for hours and can't get to sleep. You can't stop thinking about what you have to do tomorrow.
3. You feel angry about something a friend did.
4. You have been studying or working, and you need to take a break.

B Pair work Compare your answers with a partner. Are any of your solutions the same?

"Whenever I have something important the following day, I make sure I get some exercise so that I'll nod off as soon as I lie down."

2 SPEAKING
Guess what I heard!

A Read these situations. Can you think of a personal example for each one?

1. You overheard someone say something really funny.
2. Someone told you a big secret.
3. You realized something important.

B Pair work Discuss your answers with a partner.

"I was on the subway, and I overheard this guy tell his friend that he'd gotten into the bathtub the night before and realized he was still wearing his socks! I just burst out laughing."

3 LISTENING & SPEAKING
Stressed out!

A Listen to Dr. Phillips talking about stress. What is the main topic of his presentation? Choose the correct answer.

- ☐ a. the stress of living on a tight budget
- ☐ b. college students and stress
- ☐ c. stress and nutrition

B Listen again. Choose the causes of stress that are mentioned.

- ☐ 1. not having enough money
- ☐ 2. jobs
- ☐ 3. noisy roommates
- ☐ 4. too much studying
- ☐ 5. not enough studying
- ☐ 6. missing family

C **Pair work** Look at the causes of stress you chose and these suggestions for ways to deal with stress. Which do you think is the best suggestion? Why?

Ways to Deal with Stress

- Find a physical activity you enjoy and make time for it.
- Organize your time.
- Make time to relax.
- Eat breakfast. Don't drink too much coffee.
- Have a sense of humor.

"When you feel like you've got too much work, I think it's really important to sit down and organize your time. If you do, you'll feel more in control."

4 SPEAKING
Tell me a story.

A **Pair work** Tell your partner about a time when one of these things happened to you. Ask and answer follow-up questions so that you will be able to retell your partner's story. Take notes.

- You met someone fascinating.
- You did something that took a lot of courage.
- Something made you laugh hysterically.

B **Group work** Join another pair and tell your partner's story.

"Maria once met a famous marathon runner at a café. It was pretty crowded, and she had just sat down at the last free table. The next thing she knew, the runner walked up to her and . . ."

GRAMMAR PLUS

1A Verbs followed by gerunds

These verbs are followed by a gerund.

deny discuss finish mention practice quit resist suggest

These verbs are followed by an infinitive.

arrange claim decide demand deserve expect pretend refuse volunteer

Some common expressions are always followed by gerunds.

She **had fun / a good time** arranging the party.
He **has trouble / a tough time** getting his assignments in on time.
He**'s busy** cooking dinner right now.
She never **worries about** cleaning up after herself.

Some verbs take either a gerund or an infinitive, but the meaning of the sentence will be different.

I **stopped to drink** some coffee. *(I ended one activity and began another.)*
I **stopped drinking** coffee. *(I don't do that activity anymore.)*
I **stopped running** when I got tired. *(I temporarily ended the activity.)*

1 Complete these sentences with the gerund or infinitive form of the verb in parentheses.

1. I practiced *speaking* (speak) English with an American friend last night.
2. He volunteered ____________ (help) at the hospital fund-raiser.
3. They discussed ____________ (go) somewhere exotic on their vacation this year.
4. She's stopped ____________ (talk) to him because they had a big argument.
5. My great-grandmother has trouble ____________ (get) to our family reunions.
6. Laura always denies ____________ (be) wild and crazy, but she really is.

2 Choose the best answer to complete the sentences.

My friend Shanda is pretty cool and very outgoing. She's usually busy (1) *to do / doing* a million things at once. Last week, I suggested (2) *to go / going* out for dinner and (3) *to see / seeing* a movie. We arranged (4) *to meet / meeting* at 7:00. Well, I know she doesn't worry about (5) *to be / being* on time, but she didn't show up until 7:30. At first, she said it took her a long time to finish (6) *to get / getting* ready. Then, after the movie, she couldn't resist (7) *to tell / telling* me what really happened. She was having such a good time (8) *to play / playing* video games with her brother that she forgot about our plans. It's a good thing I'm the laid-back type!

1B Noun clauses after *be*

***The downside of*, *the upside of*, *the hard part about*, *the good thing about*, *the only thing about*, *the trick to*, *the secret to*, and *one difficulty with* are used in complex phrases that introduce noun clauses after *be*.**

The downside of sharing a bedroom is (that) it's hard to have any privacy.
The hard part about being a twin is (that) people are always calling you by the wrong name.
The trick to living in a crowded house is (that) you have to find a private space of your own.
One difficulty with being the youngest is (that) everyone is always telling you what to do.

The phrases ending with a preposition can be followed by a gerund phrase, *not* + a gerund phrase, or a noun phrase.

The secret to **getting along with your siblings** is (that) you have to respect their privacy.
The good thing about **not being in a big family** is (that) you always get to choose what's on TV.
The upside of **a large family** is (that) you always have someone to spend time with.
The only thing about **working moms** is (that) they have less time to spend with you.

1 Complete the sentences with *about*, *of*, *with*, or *to*.

1. The best thing ___*about*___ my grandmother living with us is that she's a great cook.
2. The upside ____________ being a two-income family is we can afford a few small luxuries.
3. One difficulty ____________ living with my in-laws is that they want everything their way.
4. The trick ____________ living in a large family is you have to learn to respect each other.
5. The hard part ____________ strict parents is you always have to remember the rules.
6. The problem ____________ not going to our family reunion is I won't see my cousins.

2 Rewrite the sentences. Change the noun phrases in boldface to gerund phrases.

1. The trouble with **a big family** is it's expensive to feed everyone.
   The trouble with having a big family is it's expensive to feed everyone.
2. The trick to **a two-income family** is you have to schedule family time together.
3. The hard part about **a big house** is there's so much work to do.
4. The upside of **a big house** is no one has to share a room.
5. The only bad thing about **little brothers** is I always have to babysit them.
6. One good thing about **little sisters** is they really look up to you.
7. One problem with **an extended family** is we had to get a bigger car.
8. The greatest thing about **a small house** is the bills are a lot lower.

2A Past modals and phrasal modals of obligation

Some past modals and phrasal modals of obligation are stronger than others.

Strong obligation: To show that there was no choice about doing the action, use *had to.* (Note that *must* is not used in the past.)
My parents **had to** go to school on Saturdays.

Expectation: There was a general expectation that an action was required or prohibited.
She **was supposed to** talk to her professor after class. *(But she probably didn't.)*
He **wasn't supposed to** drive the car to school. *(But he probably did.)*

Advisability: There was a good idea or a correct action in a particular situation, but it was or was not done.
He **should have** taken better notes in class. *(But he didn't.)*
She **shouldn't have** bought such an expensive jacket. *(But she did.)*

Necessity: The action was considered to be necessary or unnecessary. However, unlike *had to,* there is a choice about doing or not doing the action.
I **needed to** make an appointment with the counselor.
I **didn't need to** buy the textbook, but I thought it looked interesting.

No obligation: There is complete choice about doing the action.
I **didn't have to** take piano lessons, but I wanted to.

1 Choose the correct answer to complete the sentence.

1. Jan *should have* / *shouldn't have* ignored the problem because it only got worse.
2. I *was supposed to* / *didn't have to* go on vacation, but I didn't save enough money.
3. Yoko *needed to* / *wasn't supposed to* ignore her parents' advice, but she did.
4. He fixed the leak himself, so he *didn't need to call* / *should have called* a plumber.
5. When I got older, I *had to* / *wasn't supposed to* learn to solve my own problems.
6. I *needed to* / *didn't have to* book my flight so early, but I wanted a good seat.

2 Complete the sentences with *(not) had to*, *was (not) supposed to*, *should (not) have*, or *(not) needed to* and the correct form of the verb in parentheses. Sometimes more than one answer is possible.

1. A: I heard Rob's cell phone rang in the middle of the test. What happened?
   B: He *had to leave* (leave) the room immediately and was given a failing grade.
2. A: You're home early, Jenny. I thought your English exam lasted until 4:00.
   B: I finished early, and the teacher said I ____________ (stay) if I didn't want to.
3. A: Have you seen Steven this morning? He's late for the test.
   B: No, I haven't. He ____________ (meet) me for breakfast, but he didn't show up.
4. A: The teacher recommends using a pencil on tests so you can erase wrong answers.
   B: Yes, and I ____________ (follow) his advice. I made a real mess with my pen.

2B Modals with multiple uses

Degrees of certainty range from very certain to uncertain.

Very certain: To show that you think something was probable in the past, use *must have*, *must not have*, *can't have*, or *couldn't have*.
Jake had a stomachache last night after dinner. He **must have** eaten too much.
Sofia was at a movie with me last night. You **couldn't have** seen her at the mall!

Uncertain: To show that you think something was possible in the past, use *could have*, *may have*, *might have*, *may not have*, or *might not have*.
Jun Ho is usually here by now. He **could** / **may** / **might have** missed the bus this morning.
Tanya was supposed to meet me before school. She **may** / **might not have** gotten the message.

To give opinions or advice, there are a greater number of modals available for talking about the present or future than there are for the past.

Present or future: Use *must (not)*, *have to*, *have got to*, *had better (not)*, or *should (not)*.
Parents **have got to** monitor the shows their children watch.
The kids **had better not** spend so much time indoors playing computer games.

Past: Use *should (not) have*.
I **should have** listened to the advice my parents gave me about having a healthy lifestyle.
We **should not have** ignored the scientists' warnings about global warming.

Choose the correct answer to complete the sentence.

1. A: Kimberly didn't come to the party last night. I wonder why.
   B: I'm not sure. She *could have* / *should have* been sick, I guess.
2. A: Where's my umbrella? It was right here by the door.
   B: Oh, I'm sorry, Paul. My sister *couldn't have* / *must have* taken it.
3. A: I got a terrible cramp in my leg while I was jogging yesterday.
   B: Hmm. You *must not have* / *may have* done your stretches properly first.
4. A: I had to ask Natalie twice to turn down the TV.
   B: She *might not have* / *must have* heard you the first time.
5. A: They said the meeting was at 7:30, but it had already started when I got there.
   B: They told me 7:00. You *can't have* / *must have* been told the wrong time.
6. A: Marnie wasn't at work yesterday. Was she sick?
   B: Well, she *couldn't have* / *must have* been too sick. I saw her at the park.
7. A: I only used your camera to take a few pictures. I don't see why you're so upset.
   B: Well, you *couldn't have* / *shouldn't have* been using it without my permission.
8. A: Sorry I'm late. We were playing baseball, and I didn't notice the time.
   B: You *may not have* / *couldn't have* been doing that. It's been dark for an hour!

3A Defining and non-defining relative clauses

That **can be used for people or things in defining relative clauses. However, it cannot be used as a replacement for *where* or *when* with the meaning "in which," "at which," or "during which."**
Many of the people **that live in Paris** leave the city in August to vacation in other places.
A statue of ducks **that can be found in Boston** is a popular tourist attraction for children.
Pamplona is that city in Spain **where the bulls run through the streets during a summer festival**.
Summer is the season **when New York is crowded with tourists from all over the world.**

That **cannot be used in non-defining relative clauses. *Who*, *which*, or *where* are used instead.**
Cairo, **which has fascinated Europeans for ages**, draws countless tourists each year.
Our tour guide, **who knew a great deal about souvenirs in Otavalo**, helped us buy some beautiful presents for our friends.

1 Complete the defining relative clauses with *that*, *who*, *when*, or *where*. Sometimes more than one answer is possible.

1. People *who / that* live in cities have more stress than people ____________ live in small towns.
2. Amy likes to stay in hotels ____________ there are lots of theaters and restaurants nearby.
3. Some city people have cottages by lakes ____________ they can swim and relax during the summer season.
4. My family and I always visit Brazil in the month ____________ the Carnaval festival begins.
5. Many office workers like to have lunch in a park ____________ they can sit in the sun and enjoy the nature ____________ is all around them.
6. The city is better for students ____________ want to work in the summer because it's the place ____________ the job market offers the most opportunities.
7. People ____________ live in towns ____________ there is no public transportation system often own cars.
8. If you're going to Asia in April, Tokyo is a city ____________ I recommend visiting because spring is the season ____________ the cherry trees are in bloom.

2 Match the information about these cities. Then make sentences with non-defining relative clauses.

1. New Yorkers / huge baseball fans *c*	a. was also the location of the first games.
2. Saint Petersburg / the Hermitage is located ___	b. is a popular winter destination.
3. Athens / 2004 Summer Olympics were held ___	c. have two pro teams in their city.
4. Sydney / famous for its Opera House ___	d. is crossed by many canals.
5. Venice / built on 118 small islands ___	e. was Russia's capital for many years.
6. Hawaii / has warm weather all year ___	f. also has a well-known bridge.

New Yorkers, who are huge baseball fans, have two pro teams in their city.

3B Order of modifiers

Shape (*round, thin*), color (*red, blue*), and material (*silk, plastic*) are also used to describe nouns. They appear in the following order:

Quality	Size	Shape	Age	Color	Type	Material	Noun
quaint	little	**winding**					streets
picturesque			old	**brightly colored**	resort		hotels
	small				Thai	**wooden**	fishing boats

1 Put the words in the correct order.

1. He bought a *red / house / brick / little* in the center of town.
   He bought a little red brick house in the center of town.
2. They're renting a *cottage / pink / traditional / square* beside the river.
3. He hated living in a *border / town / remote / little* with its *wooden / houses / run-down.*
4. The town had many *old / buildings / cement* with *steel / dirty / black / roofs.*

3B Connecting contrasting ideas

There are three ways to connect contrasting ideas.

To begin an adverb clause, use *although* or *even though.*
I'd like to live in a small town someday **even though** I love all the opportunities in big cities.
Although I love all the opportunities in big cities, I'd like to live in a small town someday.

To begin an independent clause, use the transition words *however, nevertheless*, or *on the other hand.* Note the punctuation with transition words.
I love big cities. **However** / **On the other hand**, I'd like to live in a small town someday.
I love big cities; **nevertheless** / **however**, I'd like to live in a small town someday.

To begin a noun phrase, use the prepositions *despite* or *in spite of.*
Despite all the opportunities in big cities, I'd like to live in a small town someday.
I'd like to live in a small town someday **in spite of** all the opportunities in big cities.

2 Complete each sentence with a word or phrase from the box. Sometimes more than one answer is possible.

although	however	in spite of	on the other hand	nevertheless

1. This is a great city; *nevertheless / however*, it's too crowded.
2. ________________ living downtown is expensive, there's a lot to do.
3. The summer is beautiful here. ________________, it's terrible in the winter.
4. ________________ the high crime rate, I'm not afraid to walk home alone after dark.

4A Reduced time clauses

In a reduced time clause, the subject of the clause is omitted and the verb is changed to an *-ing* form. A time clause with *before*, *after*, or *while* can be reduced only if the subject in the sentence's other clause is the same.
Before **I go to sleep**, I like to read.
Before **going to sleep**, I like to read.
I like to read before **going to sleep**.
Before **the baby goes to sleep, his mother reads** to him.

***Once*, *every time*, *till*, *as*, *the first / next / last time*, and many other time expressions can be used in time clauses. Time clauses beginning with these expressions cannot be reduced.**
As soon as / **Once** I drink that first cup of coffee, I'm ready for the day.
Whenever / **Every time** I stay out late, I have trouble getting up the next morning.
I always stay at the office **until** / **till** I've finished all my work.
I like to watch TV **as** I'm eating dinner.
The last time I drank too much coffee, I was jittery all day.

1 Which of these time clauses can be reduced (*R*)? Which ones cannot be reduced (*N*)? Write the correct letter.

_N_ 1. Ever since I can remember, I've been a night owl.
____ 2. Once I fall asleep, I almost never wake up until morning.
____ 3. My mother races off to work right after I leave for school.
____ 4. Every time Jerry comes to visit, he keeps me up past my bedtime.
____ 5. As soon as I get up in the morning, I drink a large glass of water.
____ 6. I always listen to music while I run.
____ 7. I often doze off as I'm watching TV at night.
____ 8. Whenever I drink coffee after 3:00, I have trouble falling asleep.
____ 9. I always have breakfast at a local café before I start classes for the day.
____ 10. The last time I stayed at a hotel, the bed was really uncomfortable.

2 Rewrite the sentences using reduced time clauses.

1. I usually watch the news while I have breakfast.
   I usually watch the news while having breakfast.
2. My sister won't drink orange juice after she brushes her teeth.
3. She does a lot of housework before she leaves for work in the morning.
4. Power nappers work better after they sleep for a short time during the day.
5. You probably shouldn't eat anything heavy before you exercise.
6. If I listen to soft music while I study, I can concentrate better.
7. After I'm in an argument, I need to be by myself for an hour or two.
8. Before I chill out at night, I make sure everything is ready for the morning.

4B Clauses stating reasons and conditions

The following are all additional commonly used clauses that state reasons and conditions.

Now that **introduces a change in general circumstances that explains the main clause.** ***Now that*** **means "because now."**
Now that I have a job that starts early, I have to leave the house by 6:30.

Whether or not **introduces a condition that might or might not occur and which will not influence the main clause. Note its two possible positions.**
She goes jogging every morning **whether or not** it's bad weather.
She goes jogging every morning **whether** it's bad weather **or not**.

Provided / Providing **(*that*) introduces a condition that must be met for the main clause to be true.**
Provided that I get all my schoolwork done, my weekend will be free.
Providing that I get a promotion, I'll stay with my company a few more years.

1 Match each sentence on the left with the best meaning on the right.

1. She always has breakfast whether she's in a hurry or not. _c_
2. Now that she works the afternoon shift, she always has time for breakfast. ____
3. Unless her mother makes it, she doesn't bother with breakfast. ____
4. She only eats breakfast if she's hungry. ____
5. Provided that she has enough time, she has breakfast. ____
6. As long as she has breakfast, she can concentrate in class. ____

a. She has plenty of time to eat something in the morning.
b. She skips her morning meal when she doesn't feel like eating anything.
c. She eats something every morning.
d. When she is in a hurry, she doesn't eat breakfast.
e. She never makes her own morning meal.
f. If she doesn't eat, she can't think clearly.

2 Choose the correct answer to complete the sentence.

1. He won't be late for work (*as long as*) / *unless* the bus is on time.
2. *Considering that* / *Just in case* I took a nap, I shouldn't feel this drowsy.
3. I'll wake up on time tomorrow, *provided that* / *unless* I set my alarm clock.
4. He jogs after work *now that* / *unless* he's too tired at the end of the day.
5. My brother usually goes to bed early *now that* / *whether or not* he's sleepy.
6. *Now that* / *Even if* I'm going to bed later, I'm getting up later.
7. I'm afraid to nap at lunch *even if* / *just in case* I start snoring at my desk.
8. *Even if* / *Provided that* I'm totally exhausted, I can't sleep on airplanes.

5A Infinitive and gerund phrases

In a sentence with *It's* + adjective + infinitive, it is possible to follow the adjective with *for* and an object. The object can be a pronoun or a noun.
It's difficult for her to talk about her feelings openly.
It's customary for North Americans to make frequent eye contact.

For sentences in the negative, use *not* + infinitive or *not* + gerund.
It's considered rude **not to thank** people who give you gifts.
Not thanking people who give you gifts is considered rude.

Adjectives of feeling (*glad, happy, pleased*) cannot be used with the *It's* + adjective + infinitive structure. Instead, the sentence needs to say who has (or doesn't have) these feelings.
Most parents are happy to see their children go to college.
People are always delighted to get compliments.

1 Rewrite the sentences using infinitive or gerund phrases.

1. It's important to make a good first impression.
   Making a good first impression is important.
2. Arriving late for an appointment is inappropriate in most countries.
3. It's fairly typical for college students to get to a party late.
4. It's considered rude not to be punctual for a dinner party.
5. Keeping the conversation going is easy for Elyse.
6. Showing the bottom of your feet is offensive in some places.
7. It's good form to bring a small gift to a dinner party.
8. Talking about politics is sometimes risky.
9. It's customary for some parents to brag about their children.
10. Thanking the hostess the day after a party is a nice idea.

2 Write sentences with infinitive phrases using the words below.

1. Tom / always happy / lend money to his friends
   Tom is always happy to lend money to his friends.
2. Wendy / unusual / arrive late to class
   It's unusual for Wendy to arrive late to class.
3. Donald / relaxing / not have homework over the weekend
4. Min / always glad / help a friend in need
5. many tourists / surprised / learn about some American customs
6. students / inappropriate / interrupt a teacher
7. new employees / often afraid / ask their bosses for help
8. dinner guests / customary / thank their hosts
9. businesspeople / important / be punctual for appointments

5B Reported speech

The modals *can*, *may*, *must*, *have to*, and *don't have to* change in reported speech. *Might* and *should* do not change. Also notice how the pronouns change in reported speech.

Statements	Reported statements
"You **can** go to the party with **me**."	She said I **could** go to the party with **her**.
"I **may** go to a movie tonight."	He said he **might** go to a movie tonight.
"We **must** tell him the truth."	They said they **had to** tell him the truth.
"He **has to** go to the bank."	He said he **had to** go to the bank.
"You **don't have to** pay **me** back.	She said I **didn't have to** pay **her** back.
"We **might** get married."	She said they **might** get married.
"I **should** replace **my** old laptop.	He said he **should** replace **his** old laptop.

***Say* and *tell* are used differently in reported speech. *Tell* must be followed by a noun or object pronoun. *Say* is not followed by a noun/pronoun object.**

Statements	Reported statements
"Don't park the car there."	She **told me** not to park the car there. She **said** not to park the car there.

When a very recent statement is being reported, no tense change is necessary.

A: I didn't hear that. What did she say?
B: She said she **wants** to go out for dinner.

Review the rules for reported speech on page 41. Change these conversations to reported speech.

1. Ryan: I'm thinking of applying for a promotion at work.
   Emma: What kind of promotion is it?
   Ryan: Our department needs a new manager.
   Emma: You should definitely apply!
   Ryan: I'm a little nervous because there's a big interview.
   Emma: You just have to practice. I can help you.
   Ryan told Emma he was thinking of applying for a promotion at work.

2. Karl: Do we have to sign up for our after-school club?
   Tanya: You can sign up until noon.
   Ava: Don't wait too long. The good clubs are filling up fast.
   Karl: I'll do it after I eat my lunch.

3. Larry: I'm going to the Galápagos Islands in April.
   Jason: That's wonderful! You must send me some photos.
   Larry: I'll send you some. I promise! But why don't you go with me?
   Jason: I can't go. I may be starting a new job in April.

6A Present perfect vs. simple past

Use the present perfect to report a repeated past event that could continue into the present.
Thieves **have robbed** three banks this year.
The seal **has painted** four pictures so far.

Use the present perfect to report an event that has an effect on the present, or is still relevant.
She**'s been** more careful since she lost her car keys.
The store **has had** a security camera for a month now.

1 Complete these sentences with the simple past or the present perfect form of the verbs in parentheses.

1. The police ___*caught*___ (catch) the robber when he ____________ (sell) the stolen art.
2. Unbelievably, the same woman ____________ (win) the lottery twice since May.
3. So far, the children ____________ (raise) more than $500 for charity.
4. Since the city ____________ (pass) its new laws last year, crime ____________ (fall).
5. The kidnappers ____________ (not call) and ____________ (not demand) any ransom yet.
6. No storms ____________ (strike) since the summer ____________ (begin).

6A Present perfect vs. present perfect continuous

Some verbs, such as *live*, *work*, *study*, *give/take (lessons)*, and *teach*, express the idea of an ongoing action. They can usually be used in either the present perfect or the present perfect continuous.

He **has lived** in London for eight years. | He **has been living** in London for eight years.
I **have taken** violin lessons since I was three. | I **have been taking** violin lessons since I was three.

2 Review the rules for the present perfect and the present perfect continuous on page 45. Then choose the correct form of the verb to complete the article. Sometimes more than one answer is possible.

It's a sad day for many who (1) *(have lived)* / *(have been living)* in this town since they were children. The town council (2) *has decided / has been deciding* to take down the old fishing pier.

Fisherman Bob Kates said, "I (3) *have worked / have been working* here since I was young. Generations of kids (4) *have taken / have been taking* swimming lessons here. I myself (5) *have jumped / have been jumping* off this pier many times, especially on hot summer days. However, today the temperature (6) *has reached / has been reaching* 36 degrees Celsius, but nobody can jump off the pier as the town (7) *has already put up / has already been putting up* barriers. It's true that the pier (8) *has been / has been being* in pretty bad condition for a while now, so I guess it's a safety issue."

It's not all bad news for Mr. Kates. The town (9) *has studied / has been studying* proposals for replacing the pier for a year now, and in fact, planning for a new and improved pier (10) *has already begun / has already been beginning.*

6B Adverbs with the simple past and past perfect

***When* and the simple past and past perfect can be used to express different time relationships.**
When I arrived in Bangkok, my connecting flight **had already departed**.
When I arrived in Bangkok, my friend **met** me at the airport.

When *before* makes the sequence of events clear, the simple past or past perfect can be used.
It **began** to rain **before** she boarded the plane.
It **had begun** to rain **before** she boarded the plane.

***Yet* and *already* are used with both the present perfect and past perfect to show that an event took place earlier.**
It **had already started** raining when I arrived in Bangkok.
It **hadn't started** raining **yet** when I arrived in Bangkok.

Choose the correct form of the verb to complete the story.

The taxi arrived to take Erica to the airport for her flight to London. Until that day she (1) *was never* / *had never been* on an international flight. The travel agent (2) *told* / *had told* her to get to the airport early, so she (3) *arrived* / *had arrived* four hours before her flight was due to leave. When she (4) *got* / *had gotten* there, she (5) *realized* / *had realized* she had plenty of time to spare, so she (6) *decided* / *had decided* to have some coffee and a snack and look at the newspaper before she (7) *checked in* / *had checked in*. She (8) *already bought* / *had already bought* some chocolate bars to eat on the plane, so she decided to have one of those. She sat at the counter and ordered a coffee.

When her coffee (9) *came* / *had come*, she pulled her favorite section out of the newspaper, carefully refolded it, and put it on the counter beside her. When she (10) *reached* / *had reached* for her chocolate bar, she saw that someone (11) *already took* / *had already taken* it out of the package and (12) *broke* / *had broken* it into eight tidy squares. She looked beside her and saw a distinguished-looking businessman. Before that, she (13) *didn't really notice* / *hadn't really noticed* him. She watched as he picked up a piece of the chocolate and calmly popped it into his mouth. She (14) *never saw* / *had never seen* such rude behavior in her life, so still staring at him, she (15) *picked up* / *had picked up* a piece and ate it. By now, he was staring back. He picked up another piece and ate it. So did Erica. Finally, there was only one piece left. Erica (16) *took* / *had taken* it.

The man stood up. He said, "Look. If you're that hungry, buy yourself a donut!" He (17) *slammed* / *had slammed* a dollar bill down on the counter and stormed out. In her entire life, she (18) *was never* / *had never been* so shocked. Muttering to herself, Erica began to gather up her things. Suddenly, she stopped, standing as still as a statue. There, under her newspaper, (19) *was* / *had been* her chocolate bar, exactly where she (20) *put* / *had put* it before the whole fiasco began.

VOCABULARY PLUS

1A Personality collocations

Choose the correct words to complete the sentences.

1. I'm thinking about different careers. Since most people think I'm *calm and cool* / *wild and crazy* / *friendly and outgoing*, I'd probably be a good air traffic controller. Also, I love planes! **–Jen**
2. I enjoy shopping and have always wanted to work in retail. My family thinks I'm *friendly and outgoing* / *shy and reserved* / *neat and tidy* and advises me to become a sales manager. **–Eva**
3. I'll do anything to make people laugh. My friends think I'm *wild and crazy* / *laid-back and relaxed* / *kind and generous*. They think I might have a future as a comedian. **–Matt**
4. I've traveled to many countries on my own. Since I'm *laid-back and relaxed* / *neat and tidy* / *strong and independent* and enjoy photography, I want to become a photojournalist. It would be exciting to travel around the world to cover major news events. **–Paolo**
5. I tend to be *friendly and outgoing* / *shy and reserved* / *honest and sincere*, so I prefer to work alone. I plan to become a software developer. **–Jim**

1B Compound family terms

Combine the prefixes and the suffix with some of the words for family members to complete the conversation. Some prefixes will be used more than once.

great-   grand-   great-grand-   -in-law

aunt   brother   father   mother   nephew   niece   uncle

Sara: Hi, Alex! The whole family is here at the wedding! Do you see my (1) *great-grandmother* over there?

Alex: Is she your mom's grandmother or your dad's grandmother?

Sara: My mom's. And look, there's Raul. He's married to Hugo's older sister. He's Hugo's (2) ________________, but they get along better than most brothers.

Alex: Who's your favorite relative?

Sara: Oh, my (3) ________________ Vera, my grandmother's sister. Although Vera has five (4) ________________ besides me, I'm probably the closest. She lived next door when I was growing up and taught me to play the guitar.

Alex: That's cool . . .

Sara: Hey, do you see my (5) ________________ Pat making my dad laugh? Pat is my father's uncle. It's always fun to hear his stories!

Alex: So, who is the other person with them?

Sara: Oh, that's my (6) ________________, you know, my dad's grandfather. Let's go and say hello.

2A Collocations with *problem*

Choose the correct words to complete the sentences.

Problem-Solving Tips

1. The best way to *run into* / *deal with* a problem is to figure out what it is.
2. After you *identify* / *ignore* a problem, analyze it and think of possible solutions.
3. It's a mistake to believe that if you *ignore* / *cause* a problem long enough, it will go away.
4. Don't *aggravate* / *run into* problems by worrying too much about them and coming up with poor solutions.
5. Sometimes discussing a problem with others will help you *cause* / *solve* it.
6. Don't blame your problems on other people. It's best just to *deal with* / *avoid* problems as soon as possible.

2B Verbs of belief

Replace the underlined words with the correct form of the word or phrase from the box that means the same thing.

1. **be positive** **doubt** **suppose**

   The archaeologist dug up pieces of pottery in the castle ruins. After studying the pottery markings, he was sure that it was from the 16th century. *was positive*

2. **assume** **be certain** **have a hunch**

   Based on clues at the crime scene, the detective suspected that the husband must have known something about his wife's disappearance. ______________

3. **guess** **know for a fact** **suppose**

   The accountant carefully reviewed his client's records and was certain that all of his earnings and expenses were reported correctly. ______________

4. **be sure** **doubt** **suspect**

   After examining the brushstrokes of the painting, the art expert figured that it must be a forgery. ______________

5. **be certain** **have a hunch** **suppose**

   The lab technician studied the tooth under a microscope. She was sure it belonged to a humpback whale. ______________

6. **be positive** **doubt** **guess**

   When the reporter investigated the story, he had a hunch that the politician was lying about the bank loan. ______________

3A Features of cities

Use five more words or phrases from the box to complete the conversation.

climate	crime rate	hotels	neighborhood	transportation system
cuisine	green spaces	job market	nightlife	

Su-ho: Where do you want to live after you finish college?

Ines: Well, I have to support myself and pay my rent and other expenses. That means I'll need to live in a city with a strong (1) ___*job market*___.

Su-ho: Yeah. And you enjoy the outdoors, so you probably want parks and other (2) _________________.

Ines: Yes, you're right. I want places to run and bike. I love being in the sun, so a place with a good (3) _________________ is also important.

Su-ho: That's true. You always complain about the cold winters here. Oh, and I know you also love trying new restaurants.

Ines: You know me so well! I'll definitely want to explore restaurants with many different kinds of (4) _________________.

Su-ho: What else do you want a city to offer?

Ines: Well, I love going to jazz clubs and concerts, so a city with an active (5) _________________ would be perfect. How about you? What's important to you?

Su-ho: I'd like to live in a friendly (6) _________________ where I can meet people. That will make it easier to live in a new city.

3B Compound terms for towns

Cross out the phrases that do not fit the meaning of the sentences.

1. Thousands of visitors come to this *resort town* / ~~*rural town*~~ / *tourist town* each year to enjoy its beaches, hotels, and restaurants.
2. This *industrial town* / *coastal town* / *mountain town* does not have many factories or businesses, but it has amazing views and clean air.
3. This *mountain town* / *coastal town* / *port town* is located in a valley near a river, with convenient access for boats and ships.
4. This *suburban town* / *industrial town* / *rural town* has many gardens that are famous for gorgeous flowers and fruit trees.
5. Not many people live in this *resort town* / *mountain town* / *suburban town*, but many people vacation here because it offers activities such as skiing and hiking.
6. Most of the people in this *border town* / *college town* / *suburban town* are elderly, so there isn't much of a nightlife.

4A Phrasal verbs related to energy and sleep

Choose the correct words to complete the sentences.

1. I'm feeling tired, and I have to write a paper tonight. I think I'll take a quick walk in the fresh air to *burn out* / *sleep over* / (*perk up*).
2. Lea taught four English classes today, and tonight, she had to run a faculty meeting. She really needs to *race off* / *chill out* / *burn out* for a while.
3. Ben will have to leave for the airport at 5:00 in the morning. He should probably *turn in* / *perk up* / *calm down* early tonight.
4. Dina lives in a town that's over an hour away from her office. When she has to work late, she often *races off* / *calms down* / *sleeps over* at a friend's place near the office.
5. Ellen invited us over for a dinner party last night. I had a great time, but I had to *race off* / *doze off* / *calm down* to catch the last train home.
6. I enjoy reading mystery novels on the bus, but if I'm tired, I sometimes *sleep over* / *burn out* / *doze off* after reading just a few pages.

4B Expressions related to sleep

Cross out the phrases that do not fit the meaning of the sentences.

Val: I'm exhausted this morning. I (1) *had a sleepless night* / ~~*slept like a log*~~ / *tossed and turned* last night. I even had some warm milk at 2:00 and still couldn't get to sleep.

Eva: Have you ever thought of going to bed earlier? If you put on some soft music and relaxed, you'd probably (2) *be wide awake* / *nod off* / *feel drowsy* in 10 or 15 minutes.

Val: Yes, I've tried that, but it doesn't help. Maybe I should cut back on coffee. The caffeine may be the reason why I'm (3) *fast asleep* / *wide awake* / *tossing and turning* in the middle of the night.

Eva: I take a hot bath every night and am usually (4) *sleeping like a log* / *sound asleep* / *taking a power nap* by 10:30. Speaking of sleep, I hope I can stay awake tonight. It's 8:00, and I still have a lot of homework to finish.

Val: How about taking a quick power nap before doing your homework? That way, you won't (5) *drift off* / *be wide awake* / *feel drowsy* at your desk this evening.

5A Terms to describe behavior

Choose the correct words to complete the conversation.

Liu: I'm going to an academic conference in Los Angeles next week. It'll be my first time in the U.S., and I want to behave in an (1) *appropriate* / *offensive* / *unusual* way. Can I address people by their first names?

Jing: When you first meet people in the U.S., it's (2) *polite* / *offensive* / *rude* to address them by using their title and last name. Once you start talking, if the other person uses your first name, then you can do that as well.

Liu: OK, I'll try to remember that. Something else I want to know – do people kiss on the cheek when they first meet? Or is it better to shake hands?

Jing: In a professional setting, it's (3) *rude* / *strange* / *normal* to shake hands. Americans don't usually kiss strangers on the cheek.

Liu: I'm also wondering how to start conversations with people I meet for the first time.

Jing: Well, I think it's (4) *inappropriate* / *typical* / *bad form* to start by mentioning something interesting that a speaker said in a recent session. You might also ask someone's opinion about a conference topic.

Liu: OK. Now, sometimes when I get excited about an idea, I interrupt the other person with a lot of questions. Is that all right?

Jing: That's OK with friends, but when you meet new people, it's considered (5) *polite* / *a compliment* / *bad form*. You should let the other person finish talking.

5B Expressions for reported speech

Use phrases from each box to complete the conversations.

1. **advised me to** **claimed that** **promised to** **wanted to know**

   A: My sister borrowed my car. She *claimed that* her car was being repaired.

   B: She ________________ if I knew a good mechanic. It sounded like a big repair job!

2. **claimed that** **encouraged me to** **explained that** **wondered**

   A: My parents ________________ take a trip to Brazil this summer.

   B: That's fantastic! I ________________ where you were planning to travel this year.

3. **advised me to** **claimed that** **wanted to know** **warned me not to**

   A: My dad doesn't like my boyfriend because he plays in a band. He ________________ find someone who's more serious about a career.

   B: My father thinks the same way. He ________________ date artists or writers!

4. **advised me to** **encouraged me to** **explained that** **promised to**

   A: Ted was late again! He ________________ he'd been studying and lost track of time.

   B: Knowing Ted, I'll bet he ________________ never be late again!

6A News events

Use four more events from the box to complete the headlines for the news stories.

Epidemic	Hijacking	Natural Disasters	Recession
Famine	Kidnapping	Political Crisis	Robbery

1. *Natural Disasters* **Affect Economy**
   Last month's earthquake and storms caused significant damage to roads, bridges, and homes. The cost of repairs is putting a huge strain on the national economy.
2. ________________ **of a Plane in Miami**
   Two men got on a plane at Miami National airport, threatened the pilots, and ordered them to fly to an unknown destination.
3. **Economy Falls into** ________________
   Economists report that the unemployment rate has risen and consumer spending is slowing because people are saving money instead of purchasing goods.
4. ________________ **Averted**
   The mayor is now under investigation and agreed to step down to avoid a government scandal. A special election will be held next month to fill his position.
5. **Experts Offer Tips to Prevent** ________________
   Each year, thousands of people go missing. To prevent being taken against your will, security experts suggest that you change the routes you drive or walk every day and let your family or close friends know where you are going.

6B Storytelling expressions

Use phrases from each box to complete the story.

And in the end,	The next thing we knew,
I'll never forget the time	The thing you have to know is

(1) *I'll never forget the time* it snowed in July. I was on vacation in the mountains with some friends, staying in a resort hotel. We went hiking and swimming every day. The weather was perfect – sunny and warm. One day, the temperature suddenly dropped, and the wind picked up. (2) ________________ it was snowing big, fat flakes. It snowed for hours! (3) ________________ that we were absolutely not ready for snow! We were wearing T-shirts, cotton pants, and sandals. Who knew we'd need snow boots in July?

It all started when	So finally,
I forgot to mention that	That reminds me of the time when

During the storm, we stayed inside, ordered sandwiches, and played board games. Oh, (4) ________________ we lost electricity for a few hours, and we couldn't watch TV or play video games. (5) ________________ the snow stopped, and the sun came out again. We borrowed some skis and boots from the hotel and went skiing on a summer day!

Credits

Illustration credits

Charlene Chua: 8
Jo Goodberry: 20, 40, 60, 86
Brad Hamann: 72
Paul Hostetler: 5, 32, 33, 49, 51, 61, 78
Kim Johnson: 17, 43, 70, 80, 81
Larry Jost: 48
Dan McGeehan: 12, 55, 76, 93
Rob Schuster: 27, 28, 57
Koren Shadmi: 36, 88, 97, 133
James Yamasaki: 42, 82, 90, 104

Photography credits

Back cover: (*clockwise from top center*) ©Leszek Bogdewicz/Shutterstock, ©Wavebreak Media/Thinkstock, ©Blend Images/Alamy, ©limpido/Shutterstock; **2** ©iStock Collection/Thinkstock; **3** (*left to right*) ©iStock Collection/Thinkstock, ©Blend Images/Thinkstock, ©Stockbyte/Thinkstock, ©Digital Vision/Thinkstock; **4** (*top to bottom*) ©Purestock/SuperStock, ©iStock Collection/Thinkstock; **6** (*left to right*) ©Exactostock/SuperStock, ©yu liang wong/Alamy, ©Inmagine/Alamy; **7** ©Monkey Business/Thinkstock; **9** ©Stockbyte/Thinkstock; **10** (*left to right*) ©iStock Collection/Thinkstock, ©iStock Collection/Thinkstock, ©PhotoObjects/Thinkstock; **11** ©I love images/men's lifestyle/Alamy; **13** ©iStock Collection/Thinkstock; **14** (*top to bottom*) ©Gary Lee/Photoshot/Newscom, ©Courtesy of Banksy, ©Lia/Listal, ©Kathy deWitt/Alamy; **15** (*clockwise from top left*) ©Jupiterimages/Thinkstock, ©iStock Collection/Thinkstock, ©PHOTOPQR/L"ALSACE/Newscom; **16** ©NHPA/SuperStock; **18** (*clockwise from top left*) ©eye35.pix/Alamy, ©MIVA Stock/SuperStock, ©JTB PHOTO COMMUNICATI/JTB Photo/SuperStock, ©imagebroker.net/SuperStock; **19** ©Medioimages/Photodisc/Thinkstock; **21** (*top to bottom*) ©Neale Cousland/Shutterstock, ©iStock Collection/Thinkstock; **22** (*left to right*) ©John Foxx/Thinkstock, ©Brian Jannsen/Alamy; **24** (*clockwise from top left*) ©iStock Collection/Thinkstock, ©Jupiterimages/Thinkstock, ©Robert_s/Shutterstock; **25** (*top to bottom*) ©iStock Collection/Thinkstock, ©Hemis.fr/SuperStock; **26** ©Jupiterimages/Thinkstock; **27** (*top to bottom*) ©Blend Images/SuperStock, ©Prisma/SuperStock; **28** (*left to right*) ©Wavebreak Media/Thinkstock, ©iStock Collection/Thinkstock, ©iStock Collection/Thinkstock, ©Comstock/Thinkstock; **29** ©iStock Collection/Thinkstock; **30** ©Wavebreak Media/Thinkstock; **31** ©iStock Collection/Thinkstock; **35** ©iStock Collection/Thinkstock; **37** ©PhotoAlto/SuperStock; **38** (*left to right*) ©Tetra Images/SuperStock, ©Fancy Collection/SuperStock; **39** ©Ryouchin/Getty Images; **40** (*left to right*) ©Comstock/Thinkstock, ©Andrea Morini/Thinkstock, ©iStock Collection/Thinkstock; **44** ©Alain SHRODER/Getty Images; **45** ©iStock Collection/Thinkstock; **46** ©Ammit/Thinkstock; **47** ©Greg Wahl-Stephens/Associated Press; **50** ©Purestock/Thinkstock; **52** ©iStock Collection/Thinkstock; **53** ©Jupiterimages/Thinkstock; **54** ©iStock Collection/Thinkstock; **56** ©iStock Collection/Thinkstock; **58** (*clockwise from top left*) ©Jupiterimages/Thinkstock, ©Creates Images/Thinkstock, ©iStock Collection/Thinkstock, ©Blend Images/SuperStock; **62** (*left to right*) ©iStock Collection/Thinkstock, ©Karen Moskowitz/Getty Images, ©Mircea Bezergheanu/Shutterstock, ©Comstock/Thinkstock; **63** ©Zuma Press, Inc/Alamy; **65** ©iStock Collection/Thinkstock; **66** (*left to right*) ©Ablestock Collection/Thinkstock, ©iStock Collection/Thinkstock, ©You Touch Pix of EuToch/Shutterstock; **67** (*left to right*) ©iStock Collection/Thinkstock, ©Fuse Collection/Thinkstock, ©iStock Collection/Thinkstock; **68** (*left to right*) ©Bloomberg/Getty Images, ©Denise Kappa/Shutterstock; **69** ©Yoshikazu Tsuno/AFP/Getty Images/Newscom; **73** ©meshaphoto/Getty Images; **74** ©Kinga/Shutterstock; **75** (*left to right*) ©Glow Images/Getty Images, ©iStock Collection/Thinkstock, ©Image Source/Thinkstock; **77** (*left to right*) ©prudkov/Shutterstock, ©prudkov/Shutterstock; **79** ©Wavebreak Media/Thinkstock; **84** (*clockwise from top left*) ©Allison Joyce/Stringer/Getty Images, ©iStock Collection/Thinkstock, ©iStock Collection/Thinkstock, ©Stockbyte/Thinkstock, ©GoGo Images Corporations/Alamy, ©mikute/Shutterstock; **87** ©Andrew Vaughan/Associated Press; **91** ©Wavebreak Media/Thinkstock; **92** (*top to bottom*) ©iStock Collection/Thinkstock, ©Jupiterimages/Thinkstock, ©Hemera Collection/Thinkstock, ©Digital Vision/Thinkstock, ©Exactostock/SuperStock, ©iStock Collection/Thinkstock; **94** ©RubberBall/Alamy; **95** ©NY Daily News/Getty Images; **98** (*top to bottom*) ©Harry How/Staff/Getty Images, ©Robin Smith/Getty Images; **100** ©Design Pics/SuperStock; **101** (*left to right*) ©Belinda Images/SuperStock, ©frans lemmens/Alamy, ©I love images/city break/Alamy; **102** (*left to right*) ©iStock Collection/Thinkstock, ©Top Photo Group/Thinkstock, ©iStock Collection/Thinkstock; **103** ©Morgan David de Lossy/Corbis; **130** ©AFP/Getty Images; **135** ©Aurora Photos/Alamy; **137** ©Cultura Creative/Alamy; **141** ©Michael Coyne/Getty Images

Text credits

The authors and publishers acknowledge the following sources of copyright material and are grateful for the permissions granted. While every effort has been made, it has not always been possible to identify the sources of all the material used, or to trace all copyright holders. If any omissions are brought to our notice, we will be happy to include the appropriate acknowledgments on reprinting.

9 Adapted from "My Tribe," by Erin Peterson, *Experience Life*, September 2005. Reproduced with permission of Erin Peterson; **17** Adapted from "Amnesia Spoils Newlyweds' Bliss," *ABC News*, June 30, 2005. Reproduced with permission of ABC News; **43** Adapted from "What Type of Cell Phone User Are You?" by Nancy Friedman. Reprinted with permission of Telephone Doctor Customer Service Training in St. Louis, MO. Nancy Friedman, President, is a keynote speaker at association meetings and Chamber of Commerce events as well as corporate gatherings. Call 314.291.1012 for more information or visit the website at www.telephonedoctor.com; **61** Adapted from "Brother, can you spare a dime for my Gucci bills?" by Janelle Brown, *Salon*, October 2, 2002. This article first appeared in Salon.com, at www.salon.com. An online version remains in the Salon archives. Reprinted with permission; **69** Adapted from "Mr. Song and Dance Man," by Dr. David McNeill, *Japan Focus*. Reproduced with permission of Dr. David McNeill, Sophia University, Tokyo; **77** Adapted from "4 Ways to Brush Up Your Problem-Solving Skills," by Barbara T. Armstrong, October 24, 2012. Reproduced with permission of Barbara T. Armstrong, Kahler Slater, Inc.; **87** Adapted from "Dave Carroll is still having problems with airlines," by Ellen Roseman, *The Toronto Star*, May 18, 2012. Reprinted with permission of Torstar Syndication Services; **103** Adapted from "Get Yourself Lost," by Arthur Frommer, *Travel Holiday*, September 1994.

Answers

Page 44, Exercise 1B: Story 3 is false.